FURROWS III

FURROWS

A GUIDE TO THE SUNDAY READINGS
Cycle B

by
MSGR. JOSEPH POLLARD, STD

FOREWORD
by
His Eminence
CARDINAL TIMOTHY MANNING
Archbishop of Los Angeles

COSTELLO PUBLISHING CO.
Northport, N.Y.

COSTELLO PUBLISHING CO.
P.O. Box 9
Northport, New York 11768

Library of Congress Catalogue Card Number: *79-92398*
ISBN: 0-918344-11-5

Jacket by Katharine Kernan, R.S.C.J.

Printed in the United States of America

Published with Ecclesiastical Permission

TABLE OF CONTENTS

MAJOR FEASTS

ARCHDIOCESE OF LOS ANGELES
1531 WEST NINTH STREET
LOS ANGELES, CALIFORNIA 90015
388-8101

To the readers of the Los Angeles Archdiocesan newspaper, The Tidings, the name of Monsignor Joseph Pollard is household. Each week he authors a reflection on the liturgy of the Word for the following Sunday. It is gratefully used by those preparing homilies, and by many others for spiritual reading. These compositions should not evaporate with each issue of the paper. We are, therefore, rewarded by the publication of them in collections corresponding to the liturgical cycles. May they be like seeds broadcast in a waiting field.

Timothy Cardinal Manning
Archbishop of Los Angeles

February 23, 1979

PREFACE

These homilies first appeared in the Los Angeles arch-diocesan newspaper, *The Tidings*. They are published here with the kind permission of its editor.

They were written in response to a layman's request for some thoughts on the scriptural readings at Sunday Mass. I suppose he felt that some insight and inspiration was bound to come his way if he could rely on two sources, his parish pulpit and his paper. I have always kept him in mind in the writing of these homilies. He represents the laity.

I have also tried to keep the needs of my much-loved brother priests and deacons in mind. The demands on their time and effort are more intense and diverse in the post-Vatican II ministry. I am immensely grateful that some have found these capsule homilies to be neither theological profundities nor profound prose but, simply, prods and primers to get the old head and heart working on their own unique compositions.

These homilies follow a basic four-frame format, and they assume that the homilist and hearer have already consulted the given readings for the particular Sunday. Each usually begins with a topical reference. Then follows a statement of the theme. Next comes a reflection on the meaning or content of the readings. Finally, an attempt is made to apply the reflections to the pastoral circumstances of our lives. I have preached these homilies in my own parish but at expanded length. May they prove useful to you, the reader of this volume.

THE TURNING POINT

Readings: *Isaiah 63:16–17, 19; 64:2–7; 1 Corinthians 1:3–9;*
          Mark 13:33–37

There are three turning points mentioned in the readings today. It is the pastoral desire of the Church that we note all three.

With Isaiah (first reading), we ask God to turn again to us. "Return for the sake of Your servants." This turning point is in the present time. We have wandered from God's ways and find ourselves in trouble. Nothing is working well in our lives since God turned His face from us because of our sins.

Here, at the beginning of Advent and at the approach of Christmas, we ask the Lord to come back among us. Advent means the coming of Christ, and Christmas means His birth in our hearts. This turning point is God's decision, but He will never fail to respond to our invitation. Do you ever ask God to come at Christmas, or do you reserve Christmas invitations for humans alone? What thoughtless presumption for a believer! Do you think Bethlehem will happen in *your* heart without *your* request?

The second turning point is the Great Return—the Second Coming of Jesus at the end of time. It is the subject of today's Gospel. The lesson does not consist in predictions and useless prognoses about the day and time but in spiritual preparedness. Elsewhere, Jesus has told us that no one knows this day and hour except His heavenly Father. And the scholars assure us that the signs given here are random sayings of Jesus appended here conveniently, but uncritically. The point at issue is our preparedness for "the day of the Lord's coming."

The most important turning point is our own. The response to the psalm introduces it: "Lord, make us turn to You!" It is the subject of the second reading.

God turns to us at Christmas in His Son's birth. He will turn to us at the end of time through the coming of His Son. What we need to concern ourselves most with is our own turning to Him now in conversion or renewal of heart. This is the turning point that matters else the other two are inconsequential for us, our present and our future.

Carlo Carretto, in one of his books, quotes a proverb of the Tuareg tribes of North Africa. "Place the tents far apart: draw near with your hearts." At this time of year we need to distance ourselves from the whirl of high-density living, sardine-can traffic, and intense relationships so our hearts may find space to see the face of God turned to us and hear His heart in conversation with ours. We are parched for want of listening to our God and half-blind from shimmering mirages in place of His shining face. We must make space and we must give Him the time. Stop prevaricating: we make space and time for yoga and football, for bingo and beer, for love and TV! Are these the only and the crucial points on which our lives turn after eight? Where is your hour with God in relationship? What does it consist of?

God speaks to *you* today in these Scriptures of three turning points. They affect your present and your future with Him. Listen and respond "while you still have the day."

Cycle B   Second Sunday of Advent

PROMISES OF PRESENCE

Readings: *Isaiah 40:1-5, 9-11; 2 Peter 3:8-14; Mark 1:1-8*

St. Philip Neri, with a touch of humor, used to pray: "Protect me from myself, O Lord; I could very well be a Mohammedan before the day's over!" Yves Congar, commenting on this, wrote: "Indeed there is in each of us a pagan, a Jew, and a Christian. Here below, the Christian life consists, not so much in being a Christian, but in trying to become one as best we can."

There is a reprimand here for the young idealist who judges his elders as hypocrites and for those Christian *illuminati* who have cornered Christ and locked up salvation in their back pockets. The youth don't worry me. They grow up, and the hypocrisy of their elders is soon seen not as hypocrisy but as the heroic struggle to become Congar's Christian.

The *illuminati*, however, grow only in religious pride and elitism. They have the inside track to Heaven; they hold exclusive interviews with God; they declare themselves "saved" with or without the Church; they thrive on "secret" knowledge of the Scriptures; and they even know the day and the hour of the Lord's Coming in glory. There is a rash of them abroad today as befits an age of change and social instability. They make hay with texts such as those of today's Mass readings. Beware of them!

These readings are not given to us to strike terror in our hearts. They are not given to us to evoke useless rumination about the day and the hour of the end. They

3

are not given us to fall into the panic of wild-eyed false prophets (of which our culture has far too many). They are given to us as a grammar of God's presence with His people; as a sequence of comfort to the soul trying to become Christian as best it can; and as an invitation to God's special friends (you and me) to "hasten the day" of the Lord's return by helping to spread His redeeming grace all over the earth.

We are called to "prepare the way for the Lord" in our own hearts (first reading). We are to "level the hills" of our sins and "fill in the valleys" of our omissions and neglect of God and man. We are to allow the Lord to enter our open-gated hearts so He may "speak comfort and tenderness" to hearts He loves so well. We are to work for the Lord's Coming—in our hearts, at Christmas, at the end-time—not as divine advents of terror but as divine advents of love and peace and glory (second reading). We are to experience "repentance" in its fullness (Gospel), a total turning to the Father as children in great need, not as rigid idealists or as *illuminati* with salvation sewn up.

Presence, and the awesome desire of our God to be with us, is the meaning of these Scriptures. They are a grammar of His presence with us.

Everything of our Catholic Faith speaks of divine presences. Scripture and sacrament, prayer and penance, good deed and gift, joy and the Cross, all are presences of God with His people. In the context of today's readings, Christmas is His peaceful presence, our open hearts invite His healing presence, and the end-time will bring His glorious presence. God is always present with us, whether as the Babe of Bethlehem or the

Lord of Glory or the persistent longing in our battered hearts for healing and wholeness.

Cycle B   Third Sunday of Advent

ODE TO JOY

Readings: *Isaiah 61:1-2, 10-11; 1 Thessalonians 5:16-24; John 1:6-8, 19-28*

Albert Schweitzer once wrote: "The tragedy of life is what dies inside a man while he lives." This line impresses me. It is spoken by a Christian genius who left Europe's acclaim behind to serve as a missionary doctor in a primitive compound in Africa. Schweitzer was the great advocate of reverence for life across the board, long before our theologies got the message.

It impresses me too because of the kind of work I do, which is not so much the glamour of communications as its liabilities. I subject myself to a spectrum of negatives—from influential TV personalities (who are often no deeper than the depth of their pancake and mascara) to church-going Catholics (whose existence seems to be a telethon, talk-a-thon, or write-a-thon of gripes, grumbles, and grievances against God, Church, diocese, parish priests, and life itself). They are Schweitzer's living dead. There is no joy in them. They despise it.

Today's Mass readings are an ode to joy and a song of joyous gratitude to God. May we—and especially the living dead of the Church—sing it.

Isaiah (first reading) rejoices in his God-given mission of bringing "glad tidings to the lowly, healing the

broken hearted, liberating captives, and announcing...
God's favor" to the world. He is a man with a mission,
and so he is able to "rejoice heartily in the Lord" and
"find joy in God my savior." He is a living gospel sent
from God to men. Are we? Do we appreciate the remark
of Philip Scharper: "The Christian must remember that
he is likely to be the only copy of the gospels that the
non-Christian will ever see?" For myself, I try to keep
this in mind when I work with Jewish scriptwriters or
with "sophisticated" reporters or with the living dead of
the Church.

Paul (second reading) asks us to "Rejoice always...
render constant thanks." The spirit of gratitude is
necessary to authentic Christian living. Most of us have
been richly blessed by our Father through His Son. Our
election in Christ is our greatest treasure. Our call to
participate "in the banquet of the Lord" each Sunday is
a joy beyond compare. Why are so many of us walking
about like a people damned rather than elected, like a
people cut off from bread rather than a people called to
the Bread of Life? Do we ever really stop to consider the
gifts we have and the gifts we are; and do we ever give
thanks?

The Gospel reading tells us that joy is the result of
recognizing the Messiah and accepting His invitation to
be one with Him. Our broken world and our frenetic
society are yo-yos in the hands of false ideologies and
fashionable fads. Behind all the noise and hoopla is a
great void. Men and women are looking for saviors and
begging for acceptance. Are we to let the gods and god-
desses of media and cult, of fad and fashion claim
them? Are they to be led by the living dead of the

Church? Or will you be the living gospel they read, pointing them to the joy that is the Messiah and the deep-down joy that comes on all levels of life and reality with Him and in Him?

Cycle B   Fourth Sunday of Advent

THE GREAT AMEN

Readings: *2 Samuel 7:1-5, 8-12, 14, 16; Romans 16:25-27; Luke 1:26-38*

At the conclusion of the Eucharistic Prayer of the Mass and before we proceed to the intimacy of Communion, all of us utter "the great Amen." We acclaim God as our Father and we render Him all honor and glory through Christ, with Christ, and in Christ. The greatest Amen of the believer is spoken here. It is our Yes to God, spoken for self, others, mankind, and creation.

Today's scriptural readings are a series of Yesses (Amens) to the God Who saves us in Christ. Let us affirm them again as Advent draws to a close and the Christmas wonder opens its stable doors to our waiting hearts.

God, through His infant Son, says Yes to all our longings and hopes. We have cried out for salvation, for healing, for community, and for love; and God has heard our cries and says Yes to these needs in the birth of "the Desired of all the ages." My Son is now your Son! My salvation is now yours! My trinitarian life is now shared with you! My love is given you in dimensions of touch and tangible presence! Christmas is

God's Yes "to men of goodwill" but especially to His elect—yourself!

King David (first reading) desired to build a temple for the Ark of the Covenant, for the symbol of God's presence among the people. Instead, God said *He* would build a temple for the people of David, "a house of David," a kingdom of the Messiah. Do you and I desire with all our hearts to build a temple for the Lord? If we do, then let it be the temple of our converted heart. Let the Lord be born in it. Let Him live in it. Allow Him to grow and prosper in it. Let the Christmas wonder be me—a temple-heart fashioned by the Lord as the modern Bethlehem of His Son's birth. Let me say Yes to Bethlehem not as a marker in ancient history but as a life I live today.

Paul (second reading) preaches the saving message of Christmas to all men. Their Savior has been born. The whole world must be invited to the manger of its salvation. Am I, like Paul the missionary, a living Yes who evangelizes by word and example? Or am I just another secularized Christian, one for whom the Christmas wonder is mostly a matter of sending cards and tying ribbons to benefit a company sales graph and to please a penthouse czar somewhere? Whose ledger am I writing my sweat and blood into: the book of tinsel or the Book of Life?

In the Gospel, a young woman says Yes to a choice and a calling that involves all she is and all our poor world needs. It is a magnificent Amen, spoken with great trepidation but greater trust. All of our Yesses are so paltry beside hers. And yet they are the very Yesses and Amens God desires of us. If Christmas is God's Yes to us through Mary's Amen, how readily ought we not respond in terms of our vocations, responsibilities, commitments, healing presences, and dynamic loves? These are *our* Yesses.

Christmas reminds us that our religion is not a matter of Noes but of Yesses. Our relationship with God is a matter of trust and love, of caring and concern, of feelings and whispers, of touch and tenderness, of vulnerability and intimacy. It is an affair of hearts in which Yesses are constantly invited and received. Christmas was the day in our history when God's love became flesh with the attraction of a helpless infant in our hands. His love took the form of a human heart that could speak to my own heart in dimensions I fully understand and with feelings I can fully respond to.

CHRISTMAS AND EPIPHANY

Cycle B   Christmas Day

"UNTO US A CHILD IS BORN"

Readings: *varied*

What is the meaning of Christmas? The meanings of Christmas are as many and varied as the readings of the many Masses for this feast day. All the Scripture readings assigned to the twelve days of Christmas do not exhaust the meaning of Christmas, nor do they fully evoke and chronicle the wonder and the beauty of it all.

Each of us approaches Christmas in a very personal way. Past Christmases have shaped our present personalities and our faith. At this time, memories flood the heart with moments of childhood awe before crib and carolers, before candles and cakes, before shining stars glistening on the frosty ground at our shoes as we made our midnight way to Mass to welcome the newborn Lord.

There, in that village of my childhood, among the warmest hearts in the world, Bethlehem happened every year. It just had to; for here were men and women to match the best of the sons and daughters of Israel. A Child was born to us; a Son was given us. He was my parents' Son and my Brother. His name was "Wonderful," "Counselor," "Prince of Peace."

He was everything the priests and teachers said He was—the Chosen One, the Desired of all the ages, the Messiah, the Savior, the Lord. We knew it, we believed it, and we loved Him for it. How we loved Him! I wondered why He was not first born in my village rather than in far-off Bethlehem of Judah. There were no overcrowded inns in my village, no darkened windows, and no closed doors. There were just close families and humble homes full of stability, security, and love. He should have been born first in my village. I knew it. But, seemingly, His Father did not!

It is all so long ago. But it may as well be yesterday, so fresh and so vibrant the memory. Each Christmas, I put aside the baggage of half a lifetime—the studies and the theologies, the titles and the roles, the good and the bad of life—to kneel my heart before this many-splendored

Infant in His manger of my memory. I whisper my surest theology to Him, the little things said long ago when I was not much older than He and all the worthwhile world was found within my village.

Lord, little One and mighty One: be born in the Bethlehem of every village of the earth that has faith in You; in the Bethlehem of every home that has love for You; in the Bethlehem of every heart that hopes for You.

Above all, be born this day with Your peace and healing in the houses of hearts divided by sin, beset by anxiety, broken by disappointment, and haunted by loneliness. Christmas only heightens their pain. Be born among these. They are truly the poverty-stricken of the earth on this day of days.

Cycle B   Feast of Holy Family

FAMILY MATTERS

Readings: *Sirach 3:2-6, 12-14; Colossians 3:12-21;*
   Luke 2:22-40

The Franciscan Communications Center of Los Angeles has produced an excellent film series called *Family Matters*. Several of the programs are concerned with healing hurt hearts and rebuilding personal communications. Others define love and family life in a multiple-layered manner. One can find many uses for this series in human and pastoral terms. It is a real gem, a God-graced gift that every young couple ought to receive in preparation for a life together.

Family matters are raised in the readings of today's Mass. Sirach (first reading) speaks to children on the need to respect, honor, and love parents. We might ask, Why? The Scripture ties the child's respect, honor, and love of parents to God's response to the child's own needs and prayers. The young people will, in turn, "be gladdened" in later life when they become parents themselves. "Riches"—the spiritual joys of family life— will be theirs for the same reasons. Perhaps there is the suggestion here that the way we treat our parents is the way we will be treated ourselves later on.

Paul (second reading) speaks about the unique "family" dimensions of a Christian community in a pagan society. We are to "bear" each other in multiple ways but especially to bear each other in "the bond of love." We have to keep repeating to ourselves the wonder of wonders, that "you are God's chosen ones," and act accordingly. This bearing of the community in love applies also to our bearing of our families in love. Paul then asks wives to be "submissive" to their husbands—a contentious issue in our modern theology. It should not be. The context of this submission is the love of God, not the pathology of psychological and physical brutality a la the hustlers and playboys of the world. The demand that husbands "love" their wives is in the same godly (not ungodly) context. Christ submitted to us and Christ loved us. Husbands and wives are to possess each other to the same depth of self-donation.

What we have in the Gospel is a family protecting its Child in heroic manner. It is a time of fret and fear. In this very trial one notes how the little family becomes a bonded, single mind and heart. Our own families can be bonded by adversity rather than broken asunder by adversity. How few modern families follow this example and this insight today!

For those of us advancing in age (and, we hope, in grace) today's theme of family life evokes childhood memories. I can say for myself that I believe these family Scriptures and the comments (though few) I make on them. I am the child of a family I believed to be quite average and quite normal. Against the backdrop of the present day, I am moving more and more to the realization that my family was an incomparable grace. I never saw our comparative poverty amid the wealth of spiritual riches that flooded our home. My parents were not bishops or analysts or theologians. But they were parents, and they were Christian to the core, and love flowed from them like an eighth sacrament of the Church.

When I was young the "pops" were singing, "Did you ever see a dream walking? Well, I did." I know now that the dream was this Christian theology of family life and that I saw and experienced it not as a dream but as a holy Scripture walking in the flesh. I wish you joy of the same dream, the same experience, and the same enfleshed Scripture in your own home.

Cycle B   Solemnity of Mary, Mother of God

NEW YEAR TREASURES

Readings: *Numbers 6:22–27; Galatians 4:4–7; Luke 2:16–21*

It's time again for New Year resolutions. Half the world will make some New Year resolutions. Most of them will be broken within the week.

Why we make resolutions and *what* we make them about tells a lot about our theology and lack of it. We make resolutions about our health because the doctor prescribes them. Or we make resolutions about our habits because our wife or husband threatens us. Or we make resolutions about our work because our job is on the line. Self-directed persons make resolutions that enhance the quality of their life and help them reach desired goals. Idealists make resolutions that will be concrete reflections of their personal philosophy of life.

All these are good in themselves but, as Jesus said in another context, "Do not even the pagans do these things?" There is nothing particularly Christian about them.

It has been suggested by insightful critics that our society is made up of people who live on three levels of life and of awareness. First, there is the level of superficiality, schlock, and slogans. Most of us live there, too superficial to see through things like prejudice, slick advertising, and "star-studded" Hollywood productions. The second level is that of confrontation, where the pain and problems of life are acknowledged but "faced" by whatever kinds of answers are given by protest, anger at God, agnosticism, and even sleeping around without contract or commitment. All very brave! The third level of living and of life is that at which we realize that the human mind is no match for the mystery of life, and we must reach to faith for the answers by which we "unriddle the universe."

Christians, I suspect, live their faith lives on three comparable levels—of superficiality, or of protest, or of reflection. All of us need to move, like Mary, to the third level. It is the level of the reflective person, and there is no discipleship of the Word without reflection. The Gospel today tells us that "Mary treasured all these things [the events of Christmas] and reflected on them in her heart." That should be our New Year resolution. We have not allowed the meaning of Christmas in all its wonder and variety to penetrate our lives. We have not "pondered it in the heart." It's time we did.

Let us spend time in the New Year reflecting on the import of Christmas for our name, our present status, and our destiny. The second reading today gives pointers. We are delivered from slavery to the world and self through grace. We have now the status of God's adopted sons and daughters. The spirit of Jesus lives in us. We can call God the Almighty "our Father." We even have a legal title to possession of the Kingdom of God here in time and the Kingdom of Heaven in the hereafter. These are the treasures worth reflecting on. Let us resolve to do so.

Cycle B   Second Sunday after Christmas

JESUS: CRIB AND COSMOS

Readings: *Sirach 24: 1-2, 8-12; Ephesians 1:3-6, 15-18; John 1:1-18*

Like the Christmas rush, the Liturgy rushes us into three Gospel passages of great variety in a short space of time. First, we had Jesus as the newborn Infant in the stable. Then, we saw Jesus as the adolescent in the temple amid the learned doctors. Today, we are given a capsule of the cosmic Christ. It's a lot of reflection in a matter of days. The Church seems at pains to present the total meaning of Christmas and the Christ to us while she has our seasonal attention and mood.

The readings of today's Mass are, consequently, an attempt to link Jesus, the Christmas miracle, with the major themes of revelation—the wisdom of God, the power of God, and God as the Source, Center, and Dynamic of all life.

The first reading speaks of wisdom. How every generation seeks it as its savior! How it eludes every generation, as greed and war so aptly testify! Our world batters itself inward for want of wisdom. Wisdom is the presence of God's guidance in our directions. That wisdom is now incarnate in the Person of Jesus.

The second reading tells us that we who accept the Christmas wonder are the elect of God. We are not just chosen, but chosen once and for always in Jesus Who is for all men and for all time. With election goes the grace of remaining elect. This, too, is the Christmas wonder. These two readings tell us precisely the "difference Jesus makes" in our lives.

The Gospel speaks to what may be the crucial issue of twentieth-century men and women. Learned studies abound—and the worlds of literature and film agree—telling us that our generation has lost its "center." We do not have a solid foundation for any of our great systems of life; we do not have an ultimate meaning that would give significance to our human and social endeavors; we no longer have an overarching vision to spur us on. As Yeats best put it: every endeavor must have its center, its ground of being, and its worthy significance. There is no center today. And so, "things fall apart . . . and anarchy is loosed upon the earth."

The multiplication of "isms," of divorces, of broken homes, of failed commitments, of frenetic terrorists and groups, of "lifestyles," of "laws dismantling the rule of law" bear witness to "the broken center." Not only are the systems and institutions "coming apart"; the ordinary people are breaking along with their psychic forces of intellect and will (the needs of the mind and the heart). Too much is unlicensed and "up for grabs," and even the minutiae of living are a daily puzzle. Truly, "life has become a riddle which blind men decipher in the darkness."

Today's Gospel is a Christian manifesto against this instability and darkness. It tells us that God is the Source, Center, and Dynamic of all, and that God is in Jesus. In Jesus, we "unriddle the universe" and we integrate our personal lives in His grace.

In summary, today's readings attempt to draw out the import of the Child "Who was born for us; the Son Who was given us." The range of meaning and power in this Child is wide and deep across the spectrum of life and the inner yearning of the human heart. As we have seen here briefly, it has little to do with sentimentality and nostalgia.

Cycle B   The Epiphany

LETTING YOUR LIGHT SHINE

Readings: *Isaiah 60:1-6; Ephesians 3:2-3; 5-6; Matthew 2:1-12*

The Bible tells us that in the beginning the world lay inept in a chaos of darkness. Everything of meaning and goodness began with the cry of God: "Let there be light!"

To this very day, man lifts himself from the slime of the deep and reaches to the stars of all his hopes and glories through light. This divine light has many reflections. It is the light of learning, the light of conscience, the light of reflection, the light of insight, the light of invention, the light of revelation. The deepest expressions of mind and heart are all "light" matters, giving forth either clarity or warmth. There is the "light unto instruction" and the heart's "light of love."

Today's Mass readings proclaim Jesus as the light of the world. He is "epiphanized" (shown forth) as the saving light of us Gentiles as well as of the Jews. Isaiah (first reading) foretells our place of salvation on Zion through the saving light of the Messiah. Paul (second reading) attests that he and the Apostles are aglow with this light "in your behalf." In the Gospel, the presence of the Magi at the manger in Bethlehem represents our call and our presence at the birth of the saving Light of the World. All expressions of light are secondary to the Light which alone saves man, Jesus.

The pastoral lesson of these Scriptures is that we accept this saving Light as our salvation, and that we, in turn, become reflections of this Light to the world around us in need of evangelization. We must let our light shine.

We need a renewed sense of gratitude over our election to salvation and concerning our call to share in the joy of being Christ the Light of the World.

On this day of Epiphany and in this all-too-short term of my own ministry of epiphanizing, I ask myself a question based on Philip Scharper's remark. Do I appreciate the fact that I am the only copy of the Gospel of Jesus that most people will ever read fully? I mean most people around me, not the illiterate of some Third World far away and out of sight. Those who read me as Gospel and Light of the World are my family, my friends, and my enemies. They are those who touch my life in intense ways and those whom I touch even in vague ways.

How do people read me? Am I the bishop and the priest whose deeper call to light others' way only dims me in a sudden concern about role expectations? Am I the spouse who still shines with the Christian vision of marriage, or have the vanities of life's psychological passages made my eye gleam elsewhere? Am I the teenager whose Light of Christ is lost somewhere in the psychedelic, or the imbalanced actor whose whole "art" is to write his name in strobe? Am I the "safe" Christian who follows along with peer group pressure and peer "morality," wanting to light up my life only with "the way things are done around here"?

I have been bathed in the light of salvation, of grace, and of God's love. I must be this light to others. I am reminded today of François Mauriac's sad summation of the brilliant and beautiful poet, Anna de Noailles. It could be the kind of epiphany I am to others, or it could stand as the summation I have refused to be: "She wounded more hearts than she charmed." May our light charm others with Christ, and may our absence of darkness deeds wound no one.

Cycle B   Baptism of Jesus

A STATEMENT OF SERVICE

Readings: *Isaiah 42:1-4, 6-7; Acts 10:34-38; Mark 1:7-11*

The legendary Albert Schweitzer is remembered for many things: his mission hospital, his mastery of science and music, his remarkable vocation from the pinnacle of European thought to a mission compound on the bank of a river in Africa. There he practised his singular Christian insight: respect for life at all its levels and in all its forms.

It was this same Christian genius who wished on all of us the blessing of finding the secret of a happy life. He said it was service to others. He hoped we would make the discovery early lest we make it at death with wistful regret. Today's readings are about service to others as they focus on Jesus as the Servant of God and the "Man for others."

The first reading sets the background for the baptism of Jesus. He is the messianic Servant. He places Himself at a distance from the aggressive lords of the earth. He will have nothing to do with violence, with the spoils of war and conquest, with justice based on an eye for an eye and a tooth for a tooth. His Person, His Kingdom, and His followers shall state the case—with their lives—for service expressed in love and mercy.

In the second reading, Peter recalls the inauguration of this Kingdom of service through love and mercy with the solemn baptism of Jesus in the Jordan. He was baptized by the prophet (John the Baptist) who heralded this messianic Kingdom as his singular and sole preaching theme.

Then, in the Gospel reading, we have the account of the Lord's baptism. It was not like ours. We are baptized unto the death of sin: He was the sinless one. His baptism was not, however, a useless gesture or merely a good example for us to follow. Jesus did not play games or masquerade through rituals. His baptism was His consecration by the Father as the awaited Servant. It was, also, our Lord's personal statement before the public of the ministry of service He was embarking upon with full acceptance and lasting commitment.

Here, at the start of a new year, we can renew our own commitment to Christ and review the elements that form the Christian ministry of service to others. In our time, the review is as important as the commitment because so many of us are fragmenting the ministry into special-interest causes and single-item passions. Others of us speak of liberation through violence and justice through terrorism, of fair distribution through piracy and of peace through escalating power. The negatives have become the positives, whether it's "the belief of unbelief," or "mental stability through abortion," or "freedom from puritanism through·pornography," or the plain old fornications (now empathic actions) which—in the words of the popular song—"help me make it through the night." As we've noted before, the public polls show an increasing conversion of Christians to "mores" and "values" once viewed clearly as pagan.

The elements of the Christian ministry of service through love and mercy are found in the Old Testament messianic texts. They are capsuled in the Servant Songs in Isaiah. They are personified and perfected in Jesus, and totally available to us in the short pages of the New Testament. There is no reason for not knowing the elements of Christian ministry or for failing to see our Baptism in Christ, like His in the Jordan, as our public statement of saving service to others.

LENTEN SEASON

Cycle B   First Sunday of Lent

TAKING THE TEST

Readings: *Genesis 9:8–15; 1 Peter 3:18–22; Mark 1:12–15*

The truism that ours is a legalistic society is reflected mostly in nonreligious areas. There is the sheer dominance of legislatures over our national and state lives and our inability to conduct private life without benefit of form-filling, fine-line-reading attorneys. Even our festive birthdays are ruined by "having to take the test," i.e., having to renew our driver's license on this of all days.

The disciple of Jesus is concerned with the kind of test that involves interior renewal. It is a testing of spirits; a discernment of which spirits operate in our lives and an excision of those spirits that do not belong. The Church leads us into Lent as Jesus was led into the desert to be tested in the clash of spirits over His soul.

Today's first reading places responsibility for the Great Flood on the spirits (demons) of evil. They entered the hearts of God's children (by man's agreement) and worked devastation on the human race. Through Noah, man enters a covenant with God under the sign of the beautiful rainbow. Never again must man allow the evil spirits to control his heart and destroy God's creation.

There is a powerful affirmation here of two biblical doctrines: that the core of the human heart belongs exclusively to God, and that there is a genuine theology of ecology. Neither the heart of man nor the creation that God spent six days in fashioning is to be ravaged by the demons of sin, war, abuse, and exploitation.

In the second reading, Peter suggests that our Baptism is a new covenant. Just as the evil spirits of the Flood were overcome through the mercy of God, so the idols and demons of our hearts are overcome in the waters of our baptism. The rainbow this time is "the resurrection of our Lord Jesus Christ." It is our pledge that this new covenant is valid here and leads to glory hereafter.

In the Gospel, Jesus is "tested by the spirits" and overcomes all their power and allurement.

23

The Bible is very emphatic on the fact that our struggles are mainly with—as Paul wrote—"principalities and powers, and spirits on high." In our highly secularistic age, we may not be as attuned to the power of demons and the subtleties of evil spirits as our ancestors were. Lent is a time for withdrawing into the silence of the heart to discover our measure in discipleship, to be confronted with the demons we fail to notice in the everyday rush of life, to discern the spirits that help us and those that seek to ravage us, and to renew our own spirit in prayer, penance, and the sacramental encounter of reconciliation.

In our archdiocese, we have many retreat centers to serve such a need. We can spend a weekend on retreat or a day of intense recollection. We can attend daily Mass with its systematic challenge of scriptural readings on the state of our spiritual pilgrimage. We can undergo the parish renewal of heart by attending a communal Penance service.

One thing is sure: each of us suffers the ravages symbolized by Flood and demon. As Jesus had to be tested, so must we. The withdrawal to the desert must be made and the demons confronted. The place is your choice. The time is now.

Cycle B   Second Sunday of Lent

LIGHT IN THE TUNNEL

Readings: *Genesis 22:1-2, 9, 10-13, 15-18; Romans 8:31-34; Mark 9:2-10*

Lent, like life, can be viewed as a rather dark tunnel from which we hope to emerge into resurrection and the light of day. The Gospel reading for today (on the Transfiguration) may be viewed as the encouraging light at the end of the tunnel. And I have no doubt that the Church slated this Gospel for today to encourage us after last Sunday's dark passage of trial and temptation in the wilderness.

However, I think the Church has much more in mind. It is the prophetic role of the Church to teach us how to see life in its true and luminous reality. Lent is not just a penitential season. Lent is a purgation process in which the eye of the soul is liberated from worldly restrictions so as to be able to "read" reality exactly as reality is. Notice that we use luminous terms to describe the moments of spiritual and human progress. "The spark of genius." "The light of discovery." "The fire of poetic vision." "The blaze of insight." "The burning bush." "The tongues of fire." "The light of glory." True religion suggests that there is only one way to read, see, and experience reality, and that is the luminous way. All other methodologies (subjective, objective, scientific, philosophical) are partial and restrictive.

If this be the case, the "transfigurations" of life and realities by Scriptures, saints, and mystics are the true and valid interpretations of life and meaning on this cosmos. The luminous or transfiguring way is not supposed to be the exceptional reading of life (just for the occasional genius or mystic) but the normal "sight" of every human being.

I "read" Abraham's crisis (first reading) not only as a test of his faith or his intense, personal Lent but, luminously, as God teaching us His Providence even in the most extreme of personal dilemmas. I "see" what saints see here—our need to cast ourselves totally into the lap of the Lord's love. It is in the condition of total abandonment to Him that God is challenged to meet us with every fiber of His endless care, concern, and healing presence. It is in the extremes of our troubles that God shines at His best. But do we wait for Him? No, we panic like that other Christian, Peter. "If God is for us (second reading) who can be against us?" And how He is! That is the insight here.

In the dark and disorienting tunnel that was their early lives with Christ, the Apostles had need of a Transfiguration (Gospel) by which they could "read" the meaning and reality of Christ. They were given a touch of His class and a touch of His glory. He, in His humanity, was given assurance for His mission and His terrible human future. God reassured Him that His saving Messiahship was the flowering of the Law (Moses) and the prophets (Elijah).

As for ourselves, we must "read" and "see" with the lens of transfiguration. I must "read" and "see"—and experience—myself, others, and life in fully human and fully Christian terms. I cannot reduce life to the preset limit of a computer print out. I cannot reduce my spouse to an object of possession or my children to a squad of expensive teeth braces and B-minuses. Nor may others reduce me to the functional level of their uses for me, or hold me restricted to the brain or the body that alone interests them. Lent is a time for transfiguring life and people to their full reality and stature. Life is not the game that hedonists have reduced it to. People are not our selfish pawns. Each must be allowed the luminous reality each is.

Cycle B   Third Sunday of Lent

MY FATHER'S HOUSE

Readings: *Exodus 20:1-17; 1 Corinthians 1:22-25; John 2:13-25*

Most of us hoard. We have a genius for accumulating all sorts of rubbish. Some of us fill our rooms with bric-a-brac from garage sales or impulsive buying. It's not clear in our minds—yet—why we bought this and that, but we'll find a use for it down the line. Others of us hoard clippings from papers and extracts from magazines—for future reference. Letting junk go is like losing teeth; so when our rooms are stacked we transfer the surplus to the garage and the attic.

Then comes Spring or Bundle Sunday, and we gladly fill trash bags with the mess.

Today's readings are a warning about cluttering up God's house with theological junk and the spiritual house of the heart with devotional bric-a-brac. They remind us that Lent is a time for spring cleaning, and they suggest the areas that need the broom and the trash bag.

"You shall not carve idols for yourselves . . . in any shape," warns the first reading. I look at my Father's house (the Church), and I see too much human adulation there. I will show respect to the pastors, prophets, theologians, rules, and laws there, but I will bow to none of them. I will allow no motion of the Right or of the Left to live with ease there. I look at my Father's house (my heart), and I see too much of myself there. I will try with love and pain to remove the pantheon of my idols of self-interest, pride, intellectual arrogance, lust, power seeking, divided love, laziness, apathy, and whatever else. I will discern the core commandments of this first reading from the dietary laws and rules of convenience, and I will renew my heart with the resolve to keep them.

I will say to my Father's house (the Church): Continue to offer neither Greek wisdom nor Jewish wonderworks to the people of God. Offer them only salvation by Scripture and sacrament. Offer them in this way the Christ who is "the power of God" and "the wisdom of God" (second reading). I will say to my Father's house (my heart): The Lord alone is my Light and my Salvation. Spend your time and your love with Him and waste no more on theological bric-a-brac and devotional deviations.

In renewing my life this Lent I say to my Father's house (the Church): Stand firm in driving the money changers from the temple of God. Only remember that the money changer is not only the heretic who changes doctrine from true to false (and who is properly whipped) but also the ecclesiastic who bleeds the poor worshiper by stipend or lifestyle above the poor's condition, and the Church herself at any time and in any place when she is not scrupulously concerned with social justice. I say to my Father's house (my heart): If your own teachers failed to teach you the symbolic meaning of the temple cleansing, don't you fail to tell yourself that justice issues are central to Jewish theology and the meaning of Jesus.

While the temple cleansing incident did take place historically, I look to the last line of today's Gospel for its deeper and personal meaning. "He needed no one to give Him testimony about human nature: He was well aware of what was in man's heart." My heart, the house of my Father and the temple of the Holy Spirit, is nonetheless full of selfish self. It accumulates its own junk and bric-a-brac as readily as our houses that need spring cleaning. Lent is the season of the heart's own cleansing. Let each of us go through its rooms and attic with the lash of conscience and that zeal for God's house which Jesus said "consumes Me."

Cycle B   Fourth Sunday of Lent

DISPLACED PERSONS

Readings: *2 Chronicles 36:14-17, 19-23; Ephesians 2:4-10;
          John 3:14-21*

Television has made us graphically familiar with displaced persons. Every war and each battle comes with its mortar flash, screaming jet, and long line of refugees. Each war, military incursion, or "border incident" leaves behind its legacy of tents and hovels that "house" the newest East Bank, West Bank, and Gaza Strip. The displaced of the earth are growing in numbers—and in the oblivion of our consciences. It is an international scandal.

The displaced peoples exist only by the dark side of their wits. They are prone to every kind of disease, frustration, apathy, and humiliation. They need a light in their darkness. They need lifting up by a savior.

Today's first reading speaks about the Jewish exiles in Babylon. They are a long way from home. Their sins have displaced them from Yahweh's favor and from fabled Zion. "On the aspens of that land we hung up our harps." The Scripture insists that the Israelites brought their displacement upon themselves. How like ourselves, sitting by the banks of our souls and weeping into the waters that carry away the broken bits of dreams, plans, good deeds, and love relationships shattered by our abuse or apathy or indifference or anger or pride! Just as the first reading indicts the Israelites for smashing their relationship with God by sin, so the second reading indicts us when we sin because God in Christ "of His great love" for us "raised us up and gave us a place in the heavens. . . ." When we sin we are saying, in effect, that we prefer the darkness of displacement and the condition of servitude.

In the Gospel, Jesus reminds Nicodemus that "just as Moses lifted up the [brazen] serpent in the desert [as a sign and power of hope to the displaced Jews] so the Son of Man must be lifted up, that all who believe may have eternal life in Him." The Cross is the power of our salvation, and its Figure is "the Light" of the world. The Light both leads us out of the darkness of our displacement by sin and "exposes" evil, evil men, and the works of evil for the Babylonian slaveries they really are.

Today, we might try to instill in our hearts the lesson that man has a strong inclination toward sin and darkness; that the condition of sin renders us displaced persons in God's eyes; that the real music of life (symbolized by the Jewish harp) is suspended while we are in the state of sin; that Babylon is the human heart in its deceits and vagaries; and that the serpent (in Scripture) can be the symbol of poisoning or healing, of man's fall from grace or of Christ's healing presence.

Let us look into the core of our heart to see what's in there. Is it Babylon or Zion; is it full of darkness or light; is it a tomb or a resurrected spirit; is it playing music in its relationships or striking discordant notes? What is cascading through the rivulets of the heart: a stream of virtue or the flotsam of vice?

It is only through these kinds of questions that we can name ourselves displaced in Babylon or at home with God in Zion. Have I been lifted up from my darkness and sin in vindication of the Lord's own lifting up in love for me? Or have all the symbols of exile, displacement, exodus, return, and exaltation remained for me just so many neat Scriptures in a Holy Book but not the graceful realities Christ intends them to be—for me?

Cycle B   Fifth Sunday of Lent

WHAT'S A PRIEST FOR?

Readings: *Jeremiah 31:31–34; Hebrews 5:7–9; John 12:20–33*

The Church has long worried over the effects of a given culture on the religious sensitivity of the people of God within that culture. I recall that a concern of the Irish novelist, Canon Sheehan, was the mal-influence on the Irish Catholic emigrant of the American (then mainly anti-Catholic) culture. In one of his novels, the Irish parish priest asserts: "They should close down Queenstown, and lock the gates!" Queenstown, now

Cobh, was the point of departure for most emigrants to the New World.

Today, in our culture, orthodox religion suffers from the increasing neutralization of moral values by cultural agencies (e.g., law, education, media) and from the advent in America of the secularist state. Orthodox religion suffers also from the increase in our culture of antiintellectual "religions." A look at one or two TV newscasts and just one entertainment hour before the tube show these factors in sharp focus.

In such a culture, one does not expect religion to rate any more as a pillar of society, or the "profession" of priest to be rated by youth as a worthwhile "career" ambition. In short, our culture doesn't know what a priest is for and, I'm quite sure, couldn't care less. Today's readings assume that we are finely tuned to the concept of priest and the functions of priesthood.

In the first reading, Jeremiah offers us the core of all his prophecy. There is a Trinity to Yahweh, a Trinity of dynamics, which shows Him as a living, loving God. Yahweh is the One Who takes the initiative with His people; He is the One Who loves His people; and He is the One Who covenants with His people. He is the Hound of Heaven. He pursues us with His great love and binds us by covenant to His great heart. He has made and remade His covenant of love with His people, through laws, patriarchs, prophets, Scriptures, ark and exodus, temple bread and manna from heaven, all aspects of Moses's priestly act on Sinai.

He covenants with His people again in "another covenant," "the New Covenant," the "Everlasting Covenant" made in the blood of His Son. This new priestly blood empowers Jesus to be *the* Law, *the* Prophet, *the*

Exodus Event, *the* Scripture of God, and *the* Bread of eternal life. All these are light and color, reflections and realities of Jesus as One Who is "our great High Priest" and "a priest forever."

It is for this priestly vocation, which contains and is the composite of every other title and function of Jesus, that our Lord is "the grain of wheat" (Gospel). This grain of wheat "falls into the ground" and is "buried" in His dying and in His death. But it "yields a great harvest" in His being "raised up" and in the many who are raised to life with Him.

This dying, death, and rising to new and abundant life is the priestly office of Jesus. It alone empowers everything He said and did. This is the meaning of the Last Supper which He called "the New Testament in My blood." It was Jesus' decision that all this priest-liness—this presence and power of the new and ever-lasting Covenant—should be among us until the end of time. "Do this in memory of Me." The Christian priest is empowered by the word of Jesus, not by his own. The office and power of the ministerial priesthood is *essential* to authentic Christianity, and there is, let us say it simply, no true Church life without it.

All Church ministries are related to priesthood and priestliness now and to the priestliness and priesthood of Jesus then. All are reflections of Jesus the Priest. It is priesthood that has made salvation possible with its source and plenitude in the One Who came among us as "the great High Priest" and "a priest forever in the line of Melchisedek."

Our culture, for all its claim to Judeo-Christian antecedents and underpinnings, has lost its understanding of the core and essence of both covenants. Because

33

of this loss, both peoples, Jewish and Christian, do not define themselves any longer or predominantly by their essential charateristic, their priestly character. This is why our culture has trouble asking "What's a priest for?" and even greater trouble comprehending the answer.

Cycle B   Palm Sunday

THE DONKEY AS SYMBOL

Readings: *Isaiah 50:4-7; Philippians 2:6-11; Mark 4:1-15, 47*

The past few years have given us a small mountain of books of "theologies." There are books on the theology of faith, the theology of hope, the theology of love. These are traditional. Now one can find books on the theology of politics, the theology of protest, the theology of revolution. I have read a book on the theology of plants, and an article on the theology of bee keeping. Some titles can be deceptive of their serious intent, like the book *Water Buffalo Theology*.

There ought to be a theology of the donkey. At least, there ought to be a few pages on the significance and symbolism of the donkey in our salvation history. G. K. Chesterton would know what I'm talking about. So would St. Francis.

I find it hard to reflect on the first reading today without the image of man's "lowly beast of burden" coming to mind. Jesus, the Suffering Servant, comes bearing our sins on His back like the overburdened pack animal we see in jungle warfare documentaries and Sierra-climbing westerns. The poor, dumb donkey is beaten on the head for direction and on the flank for motion. The Suffering Servant says: "I gave my back to those who beat me . . . and my face I did not shield from their buffeting. . . ."

The second reading tells us that Jesus put aside His glory with the Father in order to become lowly like us. "He emptied Himself, taking the form of a slave"—our slave. He "humbled Himself, obediently accepting death, even death on a cross!" Jesus is symbolized by the donkey in that He becomes the lowliest of His class, is reduced to suffering and silence, carries the packed weight of our sins, is beaten, cursed, and spat upon, is goaded by ridicule, and is annihilated on a Cross in a graveyard of bones. Like the faithful and silently suffering donkey, He is worked to death and discarded without a thought on the heap that was Golgotha—the place of skulls and bones.

When Jesus entered Jerusalem He did so on a donkey (Gospel). In worldly eyes, He ran the risk of personal caricature when He chose a donkey to bear Him. He came in triumph. What are we to learn from His riding a donkey instead of the triumphant conqueror's stallion? And from the waving palm branches in place of the hero's laurels? And from the cut reeds, from the fields of the poor, spread as triumphal carpet at the donkey's feet in place of the best-woven rugs and scented flowers? We are to learn the personality of Jesus, the meaning of His Kingdom, and true fellowship with Him.

We are to learn to be totally humble, open, and responsive to the will of our Father. We are to learn service to our brothers and sisters to the point of grave wounding. We are to learn the personal enfleshment of truth, justice, love, and peace rather than theologies of them. We are to learn the Kingdom's need for fidelity in each of us to the point of life's end.

Maybe there is something else. Running deep in salvation history is the openness of the lowly and the poor to prophecy and to God's word. There is the suggestion that the powerful have their own privileged supports but the poor, having only children and donkeys, need God. Dependency on the Father is reflected by the poor and by the children whom Jesus loved so much. No wonder He first preached the Good News to the poor and told the Apostles that the child possesses His Kingdom. The donkey fits well with the poor who rely on him and the children who joyride him.

I'm not at all surprised that Jesus chose the donkey to carry Him in triumph amid the poor and the children. Of the one is the earth inherited; of the other is the Kingdom possessed. He also made the point well, through the donkey, about His own silence and suffering for us, and the packs on His beaten back that are our all-too-easy sins.

Cycle B   Holy Thursday

"THE TRADITION I RECEIVED . . ."

Readings: *Exodus 12:1-8, 11-14; 1 Corinthians 11:23-26; John 13:1-15*

For priests, this Supper Mass is full of significance and memory. They read their identity from this evening and trace their holy and ancient Order to this night. There is an intimacy to this Mass tonight for all true believers, and intimacy might well be the theme we stress in our homily.

It is a night on which I tend to speak to young people about the supreme importance of the Mass. I speak of it as *the* most intense and significant moment of intimacy between Jesus and His special friends. The young crave an identification with intimacy, and here Intimacy Himself gathers His dearest and closest friends about Him. I simply cannot "know Him more clearly, nearly, and dearly" than by participating in His unique Supper.

Paul tells us that he is passing on to us "the tradition I received from the Lord." It is the tradition that we must break the bread and share the cup of salvation. It is the tradition of the Lord saying that the true disciple cannot be an authentic follower apart from the Eucharist, and that we simply *must* "Do this in memory of Me"!

It is good for the young to pray privately, or with a few friends, or on the beach; to read the Scriptures, rap from the soul, and meet Jesus on mountaintops. But nothing is ever better than meeting Him where He is most present and most intimate, and that is in the Mass. "Do *this* in memory of Me" even as you do all else and before you do anything else. It is the Lord's own command that we hearken to when we attend Mass. It is His own invitation we must respond to.

He has set the table and set the context in which He will meet His own at the deepest encountering level. That is why I "go to Mass" and why I will always insist on the primacy of the Mass. "The tradition I received from the Lord . . . Eat . . . Drink . . . Do *this* in memory of Me"!

Cycle B   Good Friday

"SEE MY SERVANT"

Readings: *Isaiah 52:13–53:12; Hebrews 4:14–16, 5:7–9;*
        John 18:1–19:42

What happened on that Friday long ago called "Good" was the acting out of the final scene of a love story, the dimensions of which are wider than the stretch of our minds to understand and the depth of which is quite beyond the capacity of our hearts to absorb.

How shall we understand this love story of Good Friday? How can we ever get to the center of this mystery so that we may be shattered by its significance to our lives and changed by its love?

No saint, no mystic, no theologian has ever quite grasped the depth of the mystery that is the Cross; nor have their lives, however responsive and magnificent, been any more than shadows of the substance that is God's love for us in and through His Servant, Christ.

Let us see God above all as Love, and Jesus as His Servant and the Servant of Love. Let all of us have done with lording it over others; let us imitate the Servant of God by our service of love. Bishops, pastors, people, all must become first and foremost the servants of the love of God poured out for us on Calvary. "Your attitude must be that of Christ!"

In Jesus, servanthood practised most of all on the Cross is the process that effects our liberation and His own exaltation. Because of this, servanthood must be seen as the heart of the Christian identity. For love is the service of continuous presence to others, and love is the continuous practice of service to others. Servanthood is the norm and service the substance of the Christian response we call love.

Let us liberate our spouses, our children, our parents, our Church, and all who have a call on us by our presence and our services of love, knowing that our own exaltation, as Christ's, will follow only on profound service. As each of us contemplates the crucifix as the pouring out of the love of God in the final act of a series of services, it is for each of us to read himself and herself as the servant of those whose claims on us are tied to our own definition as imitators of Christ.

"Behold, my Servant" must be said of me, not only by the Father and those I love, but also by the scoffers and the ingrates who "know not the man."

EASTER SEASON

Cycle B   Easter Sunday

EMPTYING TOMBS

Readings: *varied*

Abbé Michel Quoist suggests that freedom must be man's most prized possession and God's best gift to us "because it has cost Him most dearly: the suffering and death of His Son."

How, then, shall we name ourselves if the Lord and Liberator be risen—and we still unresurrected in the tombs of our sins? What shall we whisper to ourselves in the darkness of our selfishness and in the web of our many addictions?

Here we are, a people proud of ourselves on two levels, American and Catholic. We are "the land of the free" and we are "gifted with the glorious freedom of the children of God." And yet, we experience ourselves, our society, our leaders, our children, our communities in terms of sin, selfishness, fear, alienation, addiction, compromise, and suspicion. We are not reacting with sufficient energy against our shackles and chains, especially the ones that afflict the inner person.

Is it too disturbing to suggest that we have grown accustomed to our many tombs, and too fearful to exit our own and help people empty theirs? Louis Evely has suggested that Easter has no meaning for us if Christ has emptied His tomb but we still lie in death in our own. And what measure of glory is it for the Lord if we do not follow Him from death to life?

We are tomb dwellers and tomb builders. We bondage ourselves with our selfishness and sins. We wrap death sheets of addiction about our nervous systems. We atrophy our minds with cheap entertainment and chain our hearts to cheap loves. We deaden our religious perception and response with casual beliefs of easy grace and armchair salvation. So very much of this tomb theology is a denial of the very real suffering of our Savior and of the magnificent magnitude of His glorious Resurrection.

Then we inflict this same tomb theology on others. We reduce our Christian homes to no better than tombs for our "loved" ones. We recharter the Gospel so that structures and gifts in the Church do not reflect the "glorious freedom of the children of God" but rather the suffering and servitude of the lepers who lived in caves in Judea's hills.

Easter and the Resurrection have happened for Jesus. Have they for us? Have they for you? Have they for me? There is always some tomb that we are longing to lurk in and some tomb we are—however inadvertently —trying to build around others. We, whether as Christians or as humans, have not quite fully exited all our tombs. The cave-dwelling instinct still lives deep in our hearts.

Today, we should face ourselves with the issue of our own resurrection. We should be Easter to ourselves by exiting all our tombs and helping those near us empty theirs. And we should ask the Risen One for the Easter grace of staying out of tombs and the grace to be His light in this process for others.

Cycle B   Second Sunday of Easter

FAITH-SHARING

Readings: *Acts 4:32–35; 1 John 5:1–6; John 20:19–31*

We are familiar with the phrase "keep the faith." It can be as meaningful or as trite as the context in which it is spoken. It passes like empty sound between casual acquaintances but like white-hot fire between intense revolutionaries.

The New Testament Scriptures urge us on several occasions to "keep faith" in our Lord, and to share with one another our mutual faith in Him. I believe that it is most important for us, in our culture, to share our faith supportingly with one another in "the household of the Faith." We need to share our unique vision of life and our assured hope of the future with one another at a time when faith is fading in a sea of secularization. Sharing our faith and our lives with each other is the theme of the first reading today.

Sharing true love and God's love is the theme of the second reading. This is done by fidelity to and faithful expression of "His commandments."

Perhaps we do not share faith and love as well and as often as we should. This failure seems to be a reason why our culture cannot take us—or our God—seriously. Faced with our cold formalism and petty love, even the little children demand some proof of our God. One of the letters in *Children's Letters to God* (Pocket Books), reads: "Dear God. Are you real? Some people don't believe it. If you are, you better do something QUICK!—Harriet Ann."

The little book of children's letters to God illustrates well the questions they have in the face of the kind of God, trite faith, and petty love taught them by silly adults. They, in turn, will transmit the same to their own children. It is we who must answer Harriet Ann, and quickly, with a real theology of God's face and Christ's heart. Sharing our faith and love is one way to right our catechesis and strengthen our discipleship.

The Gospel teaches us that our scientific culture should be responded to in proper terms, not by a casual "praise Jesus" but with a persuasive apologetic. Jesus did not leave Doubting Thomas in "scientific" darkness with only the hearsay testimonials of "The Lord is risen." Rather, on Thomas's terms, He said: "Put your fingers into My hands; put your hand into My side. And be not unbelieving. Believe!"

When we are located in a culture of hard technology and human loneliness, it becomes imperative to render the Risen Lord as present as possible in our communities. The "bond of love and unity"—the Spirit —can hardly offer His consolation if we are absent from one another by poor community and no community. The signs of our times seem to point decisively to our need for community building, shared faith and love, shared testimony, shared vision of the moment, and shared hope of our unique future in the Risen Lord.

There is so much we can do and experience in true discipleship and vibrant community. But our structures and theologies have a long way to go. They, and we, might do well to take the TV commercial seriously when we put it in the context of today's first reading on community: "How's your love life?" How is your shared life? How is your Christian community life? What kind of God, faith, and love are you offering and receiving? I think Harriet Ann wants to know—and quick!

Cycle B   Third Sunday of Easter

WITNESS FOR THE DEFENSE

Readings: *Acts 3:13-15, 17-19; 1 John 2:1-5; Luke 24:35-48*

When Jesus was tried, there were many witnesses for the prosecution and very few for the defense. The theme of this Sunday's readings at Mass is witness: witness for the defense. We are told by Peter that we are Christ's witnesses. In the Gospel, Our Lord himself says that we are to be witnesses to His Resurrection and Messiahship.

All that we are to witness in regard to Jesus is found in its fullness in the Catholic faith. But something is wrong today. Why are there so few converts to the Faith? Perhaps the question should be: whatever happened to the old zeal and the old conviction about sharing our faith with others? Not only are we not making many converts, we are losing Catholics every day to all sorts of seemingly intense, relevant, and satisfying spiritual experiences.

Reasons for our crux are offered every day: a divided Church; a dispirited clergy; a visitation of God on our recent smugness; a crisis of faith; the sexual revolution; advancing materialism; the general fragmentation of Western civilization, and so on. It might be more to the point to suggest that we are a very disorganized Church, with an almost total lack of pastoral planning and priority setting on the national, diocesan, and parish levels. Jesus spoke of a necessary worldly wisdom. I believe it has to do with presenting the saving message according to people's needs. We call that pastoral planning.

Our first witness is to the fact that the defenseless One has become the glorified One. Jesus has been God's servant and God has glorified Him. The world disowns Him in its ignorance. We can rectify that. We too, for all our religiousness and protestations, have shared in putting to death the Author of life. We witness that by our sins, but we can counter witness now by repentance and conversion of heart. We can redeem the time for ourselves and for others by our present, grace-filled witnessing.

Yes, we are called to witness to our Faith and to attract others to its fullness in the community of the Catholic Church. We should not overstress argument and reasoning in the conversion process. It is the quality of our lifestyle that really attracts others. People did not go out into the desert after John the Baptist to hear a spate of oratory or to follow a reed shaking in the wind of doubt and moral hesitation. They did not follow Jesus for His personality but for the fact that God's presence was clearly in all He said and did. And He said what He said and did what He did as the Servant of others' need.

When we become servants of the word of God and of others' needs, we reach out that power and attractive grace that gather many into the Church. This is the kind of witness we need. But first, we must resurrect with the Risen Christ by emerging from our tombs of sin, bad habits, confusion, misdirection, and disbelief. Pray for your resurrection from these tombs so that you may witness to the Lord's Resurrection by the proof of your own.

Cycle B   Fourth Sunday of Easter

THE GOOD SHEPHERD

Readings: *Acts 4:8-12; 1 John 3:1-2; John 10:11-18*

We are saved by Jesus. There is no other saving name for us. This Sunday's readings at Mass profess this fact under the image of the Good Shepherd.

In the past, preachers and teachers often took the theme of the Good Shepherd as the high point of their sentimental discourse on Christ. They spoke a lot about the gentle Jesus, about His concern and care for us, and about His arm and shepherd's crook protecting us from every conceivable form of suffering and loneliness. But this Good Shepherd theology of yesteryear needs a little demythologizing. It breaks down for too many people in the hassle of modern anxiety.

We have led our people to believe that the Good Shepherd is some symbol of gigantic insurance against every item of pain, anxiety, and crisis. The lesson of the Good Shepherd who lays down His life for the sheep is altogether different. Jesus was slain by crisis and slain in crisis. He did not avert crisis for Himself and does not now for us. Rather, we have a Shepherd who leads us into crisis, cross, and death—and beyond them. That is His shepherding. Even as the Good Shepherd, Christ remains dominantly the model and exemplar of how to live life, endure crisis—and pass triumphantly through death.

A second lesson from the Good Shepherd is the lesson about intimacy. Take the closest-knit relationship you have—as pastor, as husband, as wife, as parent, as friend. Can you say of this relationship what Jesus says: "I know mine and mine know me"? Can you say it with the same intensity of Jesus? Judging from the rate of fled pastors, broken homes, generation gaps, and wife beatings, it is doubtful. Let's face it: is not even our deepest intimacy full of holes and gaps? What reserves we display in regard to those we say we know and love! What silences we mete out to them every day! What games we play to manipulate their love and their time and their attention! And what about all the masks we wear before our accusers and even in the presence of our defenders? We are a long way from that intimacy in which the Good Shepherd holds us. Could we ever bear the transparency of love that was His in our regard on the Cross?

We are slow to love and quick to forget. It is so easy for us to forget someone even after years of friendship or intimacy. Parents and friends are long forgotten in cemeteries and rest homes. They scarcely rate the price of a letter or an occasional phone call in our frantic budget. What a commentary on our intimacy and on our Christianity!

The Good Shepherd was different. He loved us unto death, and it doesn't end there. Our memory lingers on in His resurrected mind. So He commits Himself to us in new presences and in new intimacies as we await His return in glory. He is present to us in His Scripture; He is intimate with us in His sacraments; He molds us to His heart in His spiritual body, the Church. He remains our breadwinner even after two thousand years. Every day He breaks His body for you and for me on the altars of our parish churches.

Let us put aside the sentimental Good Shepherd and look at the real one. Let us learn from Him about the crisis we are undergoing, or the intimacy we are faking, or the presences we are refusing Him and others beside us.

Cycle B   Fifth Sunday of Easter

THE PRUNING KNIFE

Readings: *Acts 9:26-31; 1 John 3:18-24; John 15:1-8*

As we grow older in the business of living, we realize that surgery is part of health. The knife enters our life. We accept it as a necessary thing to remove a tonsil or an appendix. We may even pray for it on a battlefield in order to lose a limb and save a whole life. The surgical knife, like the scriptural word, is a two-edged sword. It wounds and it heals. It wounds only to heal.

The scriptural readings at Mass this Sunday are the same. They express the two-edged sword; the surgical knife. To use Jesus' image, they are the pruning knife of the Kingdom of God. "I am the true vine and my Father is the vinegrower. He prunes away every barren branch, but the fruitful ones He trims clean to increase their yield." We are the Vine's branches. The Father is the Judge and Dresser who daily estimates the quality of the branches that adhere to Jesus, the Vine.

Can we know which of us the Father is eliminating and which He is trimming with the pruning knife? Yes, we can. One judges oneself by the yardstick of the Scriptures. Here are a few judgment passages: being "at peace"; "making steady progress in the fear of the Lord"; "enjoying the increased consolation of the Holy Spirit." These yardsticks are named in the first reading. Am I at peace with God and grace, or am I at peace with Satan and sin? Am I making steady progress in the fear of the Lord, or is my progress steady in the fear of the world, anxiety for riches, stability before the board of directors? Am I enjoying the consolation of the Spirit or is my consolation in my greed, my lust, my fame, my honors, and the adulation of others' eyes?

The second reading also speaks of being "at peace." In this case, peace is actional: it means doing the truth and doing love rather than theologizing about them and talking about them. On the level of conscience, there is the great reminder that our appeal to private conscience does not necessarily vindicate our beliefs or our actions. God is "greater than our hearts" and He is not impressed by a conscience that ignores the commandments of His Son. We may fault ourselves, these days, with a great thirst to follow the "commandments" of each passing seer and sociologist while wilting in inactivity before the commandments of Jesus.

The Gospel reading, of course, makes a clear distinction between the camp follower and the true disciple. Jesus has no interest in the former. He is simply a tare, a weed that must be tolerated until the Day of Reckoning. Reading the signs of our times in polls, television exposes, and wars among Christians, the impression is given of a Church almost smothered with "nominal" and "cultural" members and struggling to validate the witness and the discipleship of the all-too-few true believers.

With these few the Father is well pleased. They live solely in Christ, and His words stay on as an integral part of their lives. The Father continues to be glorified through them in their bearing much fruit.

The pruning knife or the two-edged sword divides the vineyard in every generation. It cuts with healing and it divides with reprobation. Nothing in the Church is beyond its reach: not bishops, not pastors, not conscience, not excuse, not offices and honors, not pledges and programs, not even faith, truth, and love. Deliver us, Lord, from the pruning that eliminates; surrender us to the pruning that heals!

Cycle B   Sixth Sunday of Easter

LOVE SAYS IT ALL

Readings: *Acts 10:25-26, 34-35, 44-48; 1 John 4:7-10;*
John 15:9-17

The theme of this Sunday's readings is love. A life without love is not worth living. A Christian life without love is a joke. Let us "love one another because love is of God and God is love." Everyone who loves is "begotten of God." The man without love "has known nothing of God." These are very clear and very strong declarations.

There is a problem. There are many kinds of love, and there are all sorts of bizarre behavior doing the rounds under the banner of love. To most of us, a child is the fruit of its parents' love. To its parents, it may be the fruit of bad timing. To some social planners, it is an additional pollutant. Some of us "love" the Church so much we leave Her. Some others of us spend our "loving" days lacerating Her like perverts. Others spend their days lacerating the perverts. It's all done in the name of love.

Well, this is not an age of reason, and, therefore, it is an age of confused and corrupt language. Hence, love in our thoughts and love in our expressions run the gamut from substance to sin. Accept that as a fact, but do not practice it. John, today, is telling Christians that the only real kind of love is true love, and that true love is alignment with godliness. True and proper love has the qualities one finds in God, qualities expressed in the person of His Son. Read St. Paul (1 Cor. 13) for a listing of the qualities of true love, or follow true love's story in the actions and thoughts of Jesus in the Gospel. When you've done this, you will have a clear picture of love and a clearer estimate of your own relationships and of the destruction of love in our bizarre, "enlightened" society.

There is a second lesson in John today. But it's only for the true believer. It has to do with what Bonhoeffer called "the cost of discipleship." John wants us to fall in love with Jesus. It is good to know how John himself fell in love. Adulation or hero worship was his first love. His second—as an aging man—was the mystical love. One doesn't reach this depth of touching the core of God without passing through dark nights of pain, wilderness, and abandonment.

So, John is not exactly inviting us to a honeymoon when he urges us to fall in love with Jesus. When you fall in love with God while on this earth, the honeymoon comes at the end, not at the beginning. First, there is struggle, pain, the pull of the Egyptian fleshpots, the Cross, and a dying that seems never to end. The cost of discipleship is high because the treasure of true love is priceless. Today, we might ask our heart "How's your love life?" with Jesus, and whether the cost is great enough to prove both value and sincerity.

We must move our hearts outward, despite our circumstances in a fearful and cynical world, toward the love of God and the love of neighbor. Jesus so moved and He asks us to second. Of ourselves we can't do it, but with Him we can. Remember these lines because they are among the most consoling and inspiring Our Lord ever uttered: "You did not choose me. It was I who chose you. And I have chosen you to go forth and bear fruit. Your fruit will endure because all you ask the Father in my name He will give you."

Cycle B   Seventh Sunday of Easter

YOU ARE SENT

Readings: *Acts 1:15–17, 20–26; 1 John 4:11–16; John 17:11–19*

Many reflections spring from these readings of the Mass this Sunday. In the first, we see how careful Peter is to replace the fallen Judas so that the mission of Christ and the Church will continue. We see, too, how a disciple hand picked by Jesus Himself is not thereby beyond the treachery of the heart or the lure of Satan. "I will strike the shepherd and the sheep will be scattered."

Notice also how an Apostle is selected—how dependent God is on our choices for the quality of leadership He ordains in the Church. The company of Apostles put two candidates forward and elected Judas's replacement by drawing lots. "The choice fell to Matthias." It could have fallen on anyone depending on who was put forward.

We criticize our leadership a lot today and seem to offer little positive correction to our priests. Perhaps the first reading is questioning us for our assumption that God is automatically pleased with whatever kind of human material we put forward for office and service in the Church. "Grace builds on nature: it does not replace it." God must make do with what we promote. For our priests, we might be "bold enough in the Spirit" to correct them, to encourage them, and, above all, to pray every day for them.

In the second reading, John reminds us once more of the connection between love and truth. A lot of our loving may not be true loving; and our promotion of the truth may be harsh, burdensome like the yoke of the Pharisees, and totally unloving. We are to "do the truth in love" and love in the quality and texture of Jesus' love.

The Gospel reading contains the well-known phrase "that they may be one." When are all the little popes and dictators of the Left and of the Right going to learn that they do not have the inside track in Christ's Church? Unity and community are essential to Christ's Church, because it is intended to be a manifestation of the unity of the Godhead and the loving community of the three Divine Persons.

Jesus says to His Father: "As You have sent me into the world, so I am sending them into the world." This is His command to you and to me. We are sent into the world to witness to it the saving love and truth of Jesus, and to contradict the world's values when these are still deceits of Satan. To achieve this mission, the Christian must detach himself or herself from the spirit of the world, the secularist spirit. One must not be contaminated by the world's lusts—the quest for power, the quest for rule, the dedication to wealth, the overreaching in sexuality that becomes a demon of depersonalization and perversion.

The world is yet captivated by the spirit of sin. This spirit wrecks the world's attempts at values, at truth, and at love. The Christian countersigns all of this spirit by witnessing in word and action the values of Jesus, the truth that saves, and the love that heals. Gradually, the world is being redeemed in the blood and message and power of Christ. This is our unwavering conviction. And we have been sent to be a necessary part of that wonderful transformation. We may, like Jesus, be slain in the process, but the restoration of the world to God in Christ is worth it.

Cycle B   Pentecost

HE CAME TO CAST FIRE

Readings: *Acts 2:1-11; 1 Corinthians 12:3-7, 12-13;*
            John 20:19-23

"Mission" is the emphasis of Pentecost under the theme of the Holy Spirit. In the first reading we have a description of the dramatic manner in which the Spirit came upon the infant Church as tongues of flaming fire. The Spirit did not come as a gentle breeze but "like a driving wind." Here in southern California, we are familiar with the forest fire, which roars through the night transforming the landscape beyond recognition. Jesus spoke not of flickering candles in our souls but of casting an inferno on the earth with the driving flames of His word, His Spirit, and His Spirit-filled disciples.

He intended to burn off sin on the earth and restore to His Father a new creation of man and of cosmos. It is for this He sent His Spirit. You and I have a part of this Spirit-flame within us even though the ravages of sin and time may have reduced it to little more than a pilot light. Pentecost is a new invitation to enkindle the fire, to stir up the grace already in us by our first calling in Christ. Just let it happen and let it be in the power of the Spirit.

In the first reading we note also that the Spirit-fired disciples proclaimed the Gospel—"the marvelous events God accomplished" in His Son. They were empowered to make this proclamation with the full understanding of their hearers and in the structured spoken languages of their hearers. Mission is the meaning of the Pentecost event. As the Spirit was sent, so we in turn are sent to proclaim the salvation of Jesus with conviction and enthusiasm.

The second reading asserts a rule much needed today. There are many spiritual gifts, but all flow from the given Spirit. There are many ministries of service, yet only one Lord Whom they express. No matter what or how many our talents, they are given for the upbuilding of the Body of Christ—which is the Church. There is no longer to be a preference of white over black or a dominance of male over female: there is only one definition. It is "I am a Christian, a Christ-follower, a disciple of the single Lord, a sharer of the Spirit." To be Church is to live equality. Do not boast of talents or attempt to hold power and sway over anyone in the Church. So many of us, especially among administrators and priests, have forgotten this. We shall be "judged in the Spirit," and the judgment will be severe.

55

In the Gospel reading, Jesus gives His peace and His Spirit to His disciples. In turn, they are to give these to others. Here Jesus spells out the mission as a ministry of forgiveness and reconciliation. One of the points we need to stress here is the fact of sin. Jesus is not talking about a handshake or an arm on the shoulder after some triviality. He is talking about our sins, which He shouldered in the Passion and for which He ended transfixed to a Cross.

He is talking about the named and the nameless, the broken commandments which are clear enough and the debilitations through which we wear down others. These latter are surfacing in psychiatry and sociology with names like oppressive structures, sin situations, and corroding influences. As a rule, these are not situations that just "happen": they are maintained and promoted by individuals and groups who are oppressors at heart no matter their professed religion, or "enlightened" irreligion.

We are sent in the Spirit to offer the ministry of forgiveness and reconciliation in Christ's name. Let us be sure we are not maintaining oppression at home while casting fires of liberation abroad.

Cycle B   Trinity Sunday

ALL IN THE FAMILY

Readings: *Deuteronomy 4:32–34, 39–40; Romans 8:14–17; Matthew 28:16–20*

Today is Trinity Sunday. I can remember when Trinity Sunday was a kind of embarrassment for me. You had to "preach" a sermon, and you really didn't know what to say about the Trinity. It seemed to be the most difficult of all the Christian mysteries of faith. People said so and priests said so. So you ended up in the pulpit quoting some dry lines from the theology textbook and telling about St. Patrick and the three-leaved shamrock. Trouble was, you had to repeat more or less what you had already said on March 17, St. Patrick's Day.

The Scripture readings tell us three very simple things about God. He is a God Who really cares about you and me and us together. He has given us His Spirit so we can turn to Him and call Him "Abba—dear Father." He has given all power and all authority to His Son, our Brother, so He will stay with us always and especially when spreading the Good News. God is Family among the three Persons, and we are part of that Family too. Everything the Divine Persons hold in common is somehow ours too . . . even the glory of the Godhead, the Source of life and love.

The mystery of the Trinity tells us a lot about what God is like "inside." We know He is almighty, and we grow up sort of mesmerized by His power and our weakness. We know He is all-just and that we are pretty unjust with our neighbor's life, wife, limb, property, and good name. So, we are a bit scared of meeting this God in the dark of crisis or in the light of Judgment Day. We know He is all-knowing and sees into the secret desires and sins of our privacy. But all these speak only about the "outside" God. Within, He is in His very core, love. "God is love." This source or core of God is so love-full that it is instantly and immediately personal and plural. It is One and Three, one Principle and three

Persons. It is community, and it is the most simple and the deepest community of all—the family.

The mystery of the blessed Trinity is, then, not a mystery about how there can be three Persons in one God, but rather a statement about the inner structure of God as the uttermost depth and power of Love expressing Itself as person, community, and family. We, too, are persons who love and who express our love by generating and sustaining communities and families. It is not the sex drive alone or the group preservation instinct alone that accounts for our communities and families. It is, at root, the fact that man is "made in the image of God"—the image of a God who is a community of Persons and a family of living Persons. How wide of the mark are those who divorce sex from family!

In this same Trinitarian theology, we speak of the Church as the community of believers dedicated to the pursuit of love and loving service. Our parishes and schools must be seriously committed to building themselves into communities and families of faith and love. Their constant study should be the theology of the Trinity since this is both the model and the achieving grace. And the Great Commission, the mandate in today's Gospel to "go and make disciples of all the nations," is a mandate to spread, by word and witness, the Good News of a God whose name is love. More, it is an invitation and a persuasion to all men and women to join the family of the Trinity through the sacramental life of the Church.

CHOSEN AND CALLED

Readings: *1 Samuel 3:3–10, 19; 1 Corinthians 6:13–15, 17–20;*
   John 1:35–42

A recent issue of *New West* magazine carries an extensive review of the life and times of a local TV film critic. The word he seems to want heard most about himself is that he is not your ordinary ex-Catholic but an emphatically "renounced Catholic."

What he charges, in terms of the utter lack of reason and humanity in his past Catholic university sexual ethics classes, may well be true. His experience is paralleled by many ex-Catholic novelists and poets, especially the Irish. However, his case against the Church has its weaknesses. What is missing most of all is any sense of Who founded the Church and what it is all about. It is the spiritual Body of the Lord above all else, and only incidentally a college sexual ethics program.

I'm more disposed to blame the critic's teachers than the critic for such reductionism. If they offered him such stringent views (as he alleges), what did they offer him as a theology of Church, and how attractive did they make his choice by God and calling by name to loving community in the Body of the Lord?

Today's readings are glorious affirmations of our being chosen in Christ and called to a variety of Christ like vocations. I wish they could call like echoing chambers about the ears of every ex-Catholic, renounced Catholic, and weak Catholic on the earth. I wish, too, that the millions of "nominals" and lukewarms could hear their call by name rather than wait for a hearing until life is ebbing and eternity surging before their perplexed faces. So many never seem to open their invitations to intimacy with the Lord through His Church until—to use the phrase of François Mauriac—"death comes to sit on their doorstep."

Today's readings are examples of persons chosen and called. Samuel (first reading) is called from obscurity to become the first king maker. He sets in motion the line that unifies the Israelites and leads to the birth of the King of Kings (Jesus). Paul (second reading), himself dramatically called on the road to Damascus from persecuting the Christians to becoming the greatest of all Christian missionaries, tells us that even our bodies have a special calling (and therefore sanctity) as "the dwelling-places of the Holy Spirit." In the Gospel, Jesus calls the first curious disciples to "come and see" and spend the beginning of the rest of their lives in His challenge, His attraction, His presence, and His joy.

We are chosen and called to these same experiences and outreaches. But do we ever hear the call and savor the choice? The choices and the calls are in the meaning of the sacraments we receive, in the word of Scripture that speaks to us, in the circumstances of life we are placed in, in the persons we attend to or contend with, in the opportunities or blockages at our elbow.

The tragedy of my friend, the film critic, is the tragedy of too many teachers and taught of the Church.

The briefest of joys and the most stunted visions are offered them in place of the visionary breadth of Jesus, His Church, and its sacramental life. Reductionism is the bane of our long history. It never did—and it never will—generate anything better than the soured heart and the hit-and-run critic.

Cycle B   Third Sunday in Ordinary Time

THE RADICAL CALL

Readings: *Jonah 3:1-5, 10; 1 Corinthians 7:29-31; Mark 1:14-20*

One of the last photographs of Pope Paul showed him, with cupped hands, calling to young people "come back to see us again soon." In many ways the gesture was exemplary of a man who called out to our world many times and was, in turn, called upon by millions.

It was his calling in life to be what his gesture signified, the call of Christ to a topsy-turvy Church and an aimless Western world. We too have our particular callings in life, and some are more important than others.

Today's Mass readings continue last Sunday's theme of our election and call by God. Last Sunday's readings spoke of this election and this call in terms of consolation. How chosen we are! How unique is my call! How favored is my vocation! Today's readings center us on the radical dimension of our call, on how intensive and how extensive is the change of heart required of those whom God lovingly calls as His very own.

We are speaking of a change of heart that shakes us to the core. The evil city of Nineveh (first reading) is spared destruction by the total turning around of its citizenry in answer to the prophet's call. They cease their evil ways totally. They "proclaim a fast" and "put on sackcloth." There are no dispensations and no compassionate compromises. "All of them, great and small" undergo the radical change of heart and full alignment to the Lord.

Paul (second reading), in light of the assumed imminence of the *Parousia*, counsels a total orientation of life and values toward the afterlife and a detachment from the values and concerns of a world that "as we know it is passing away."

Jesus, in the Gospel, cries out: "The kingdom of God is at hand. Reform your lives and believe in the good news!" He is not calling for Band-Aid renewal of life or for so simple a reformation as the touch of Lent here and a coin of alms to the poor there. He is calling for a total change of heart, a revolution in our neighborly outreach, a smashing of personal egotism to shreds, and a shattering of all the idols on the altar of our hearts. He calls us to be the "new Adam" and the "new creation."

Radical is the only name for this change of heart. It strikes at our very core selves and shakes us to our dearest foundations. We must be "born again," turned right around, and passed like metal through the Refiner's fire.

Such is this call of the true Christian. How many have heard it? How many have answered it? It is hard to say in an age of churches filled with nominal millions who were "born to the Faith" but have yet to come to the Faith. Each of us can speak only for himself or herself. My discipleship with the Lord is very much a matter of whether or not I have heard the radical call and answered it within its radical dimension.

Cycle B   Fourth Sunday in Ordinary Time

THE PROPHET AND OTHERS

Readings: *Deuteronomy 18:15-20; 1 Corinthians 7:32-35;*
Mark 1:21-28

Religion (and what passes for religion) has been big news in recent months. Unfortunately, the "good news" of religion has been overshadowed by the headlines of false prophets and phony cults. It is really a shame that outright pathology and criminality can pass for religion in this land, that sick minds can command loyalties and criminal hearts can sell certificates of "ordination."

Jesus warned the beginning Church of false prophets and false ideologies—especially to be found in leaders claiming to speak and act "in My Name." The history of Christianity is in part the history of a succession of break away bishops, priests, prophets, and sundry gurus out to "reform" and reduce both Christ and His message to the limit of their private theologies or personal pathologies. Even within the Church we are always subject to the threat of some "visionary" or officeholder who has "special insights" into the need for some radical liberation or some new inquisition.

Today's first reading gives us God's own promise that He will raise up another Moses who will speak "My words" and tell the people "all that I command him." This authentic and final prophet is identified in today's

63

Gospel reading as Jesus of Nazareth—"the Holy One of God." He teaches "with a spirit of authority." We, who are "in Christ," need look no further for prophet or prophecy. Yet many of us do. It is said that Catholics and other Christians are the bulk of the followers of the modern cults and gurus.

It may be that there are many reasons why we drift from the Lord. Each of us should examine how clearly, nearly, and dearly we know the Lord by prayer, Scripture, and sacrament, lest superficial hurts drive us to seek our salvation elsewhere. Pastors, parents, and peer leaders might examine their exercise of authority in the Church and over others. Holding office no longer impresses young or old, nor do Roman collars, rings, and a rash of religious (but academic) degrees. Authority in the Church is an office and a charism of service. It should be exercised only by the true disciple of Jesus and *His* Gospel. This is the only authenticity that matters.

Paul (second reading) suggests celibacy as a help to free and full service of the Gospel and as a more exact sign of Christ's own condition and of the Kingdom in its final composition "where they neither marry nor are given in marriage."

Men and women have a strange capacity for surrendering substance for shadow, for turning in goals and dreams a few steps before their realization, for playing on the surface of things instead of plunging down deep. Such is the state of millions of Christians. No wonder they have not found what they're looking for. And in an age of antiheroes and celluloid personalities, they fall at the feet of a parade of "prophets" strutting across the stage of contemporary life.

In what measure have we failed to witness the one, true, saving Prophet to them? And how closely is this failure tied to the inauthenticity and shallowness of our exercise of authority, teaching, witnessing, and discipleship done more in our own name than in His?

In today's Gospel the unclean spirit asks: "What do you want of us, Jesus of Nazareth? Have you come to destroy us?" Indeed, He has! We are still infected with the spirits and demons of the self-established prophet and prophecies. Each of us must identify his own and allow them to wither before the fire of God's final Prophet and His Gospel of saving word and sacrament.

Cycle B   Fifth Sunday in Ordinary Time

SCRIPTURES FOR THE BROKEN-HEARTED

Readings: *Job 7:1-4, 6-7; 1 Corinthians 9:16-19, 22-23;*
          Mark 1:29-39

Franz Kafka is well known to students of literature as the Bohemian who wrote so witheringly of the absurdity of life, its paradoxes, and its problems. Most of our contemporary treatment (in film, novel, and TV) of the harshness of life and its "reality" of sex and violence, power, war, and injustice is a page stolen more from Kafka's insight than from life experienced.

If Kafka's eye is only darkness, at least he had a touch of comedy and a slight ray of hope. One must go to (of all places!) the Bible for a view of life and reality that is literally "the pits." I mean the Book of Job, with its devastated figure of a man sitting on a dunghill.

This (Job) is our first reading today. "Is not man's life on earth a drudgery? . . . I have been assigned months of misery . . . the night drags on . . . my days . . . come to an end without hope. . . ." Job was a wealthy man but also a very pious and religious man. He had family, friends, security, prestige, and the immense power of money. He was shorn of all this with a passion and a brutality that is frightening. He was left mumbling a black despair on the dunghill.

Paul (in the second reading) speaks of some of the pain and price demanded of one who preaches and practices the Gospel of Jesus faithfully. Jesus (in the Gospel) suffers some of the cost involved in being at the beck and call of the public. "They said: everyone is looking for You." The ones who most sought out Jesus were the ones who have best right to be Kafkaesque about life and reality—the diseased and the brokenhearted.

These are the ones (and not our comfortable novelists and script writers) who really know and experience the "reality" of life, its many paradoxes, and its failed hopes. These are the chronically poor, the crippled of other men's wars and economic empires, the illiterate of many lands (and our own), the migrants without advocacy, the children abused. And since both poverty and hope can be relative, we can include the impoverished and the brokenhearted of failed marriages, failed homes, failed neighborhoods, and failed hopes.

Job teaches us how devastating life can be for men and women in the clutch of sin and Satan and in the absence of God's supportive providence. Jesus teaches us the emptiness of viewing harsh realities with just a Hollywood Report or a Kafkaesque eye. In the Gospel we notice that He has only one response to the crippled and the brokenhearted who are "looking for You." Outreach. Comforting, compassionate, healing outreach.

There are Scriptures and there are scriptures. God speaks many words to His children. Jesus today speaks the Scripture of healing outreach. We, being the Body of the Lord, must speak similar scriptures of outreach, compassion, comfort, presence, and healing. We are the comforting words and the healing hands of God in our generation and to our own problems. Let us search out ways to soften life's harshness for others and to be their healers and their hope. It seems to me that the Holy Scriptures are of faint value if they never become incarnated in us. Jesus did not just speak Scripture; He *was* Scripture in each fiber and through every action. And while we are becoming living scriptures of help and hope to others, let us thank our God for the members of the healing professions whose lives as doctors, nurses, and skilled healers so closely follow Our Lord's. It must be their particular pain to be regarded as members of a secular profession when they are so integrally and so powerfully a ministry of God's healing to His own broken creation and brokenhearted children.

LEVELS OF HEALING

Readings: *Leviticus 13:1-2, 44-46; 1 Corinthians 10:31-11:1;*
        Mark 1:40-45

Priests, in our time, are embarked on a variety of educational programs. They call this venture various names. They speak of recycling themselves and putting a new cut on their theological suit.

Their casual descriptions hide an intensity of purpose. They are not involved with pet programs from a night-school catalog or with the luxury of enrolling in some program of studies to while away empty time. They attend courses and seminars on spiritual renewal and pastoral awareness. They find themselves confronted and challenged in their vocation and ministry.

All is geared to depth of vocation and more adept ministration of the Lord's love and grace to the People of God. The many forms of healing are part of this ministry.

Each reading today, whether by default or affirmation, says something about the ministry of healing. In the first reading, we have the Israelite community expelling lepers. In the Gospel, we have Jesus curing a leper and returning him to the community. In the second reading, Paul suggests that we even give up freedom and legitimate choices in order not to wound our weaker brothers and sisters.

Where Moses ordered quarantine of the lepers, Jesus cures them. Where Moses excommunicated these poorest of the poor, Jesus incorporates them in the community. We are being told, "Behold, a greater than Moses is here!"—greater in salvation and greater in healing ministry.

More is implied. The New Covenant in Christ is more reflective of Yahweh's concern for the poor than the old covenant based on the Law of Moses. Christ is the power of God unto healing, where Moses can only quarantine but not cure. And the healing of Christ that lies deeper than the physical cures is the healing of sin, the healing of hearts, and the healing of all creation that fell in Adam.

Today, we might reflect a little on the healing Christ has been for us and the healing we are in our turn for others. There are so many levels and so many possibilities. Perhaps our time is more afflicted by addictions than other ages. Perhaps the afflictions of battered and abused children anger us in our helplessness. We can at least support those who heal in these areas, their institutions and their programs. On many levels we can cure by intervention and prevention, by warning and by exhortation. Healing has many levels and many approaches. Some are always in our range.

Being wounded ourselves by sin, we are always in need of healing. The sacrament of penance has been described as a healing embrace of God. How often and how well do we recognize our woundedness and draw the arm of God's healing embrace about us?

These, and other questions, should be on our minds today as the word of God suggests to us the healing that is Christ, the healings we may need, and the forms and expressions of healing we can be for others.

Cycle B   Seventh Sunday in Ordinary Time

REMEMBER TO SAY "YES!"

Readings: *Isaiah 43:18–19, 21–22, 24–25; 2 Corinthians 1:18–22;*
Mark 2:1–12

Until recently, Angie and Burt were coming across the TV commercial with the cool confidence of cubed ice in a tall glass. "Yes. . . to Martini & Rossi on the rocks, say Yes . . . !" Every commercial wants you to say Yes to its product. And for all we say about "those dumb ads," it seems the viewer does say Yes more often than not.

What about this product called salvation? From a Bible perspective it seems that God is forever saying Yes to us and we forever saying No to Him. Take the readings for today.

In the first reading, God speaks to the Israelites through the prophet. It is not enough that they should remember the Yes He spoke to them in the Exodus from Egypt. They must now notice and celebrate the fact that He is saying Yes once again in a new exodus, the exodus from Babylon. The in-between time has been spent by them in sins, i.e., in saying No. No to His commandments. No to His many loving presences. No to His exclusive embrace. God's Yes has been answered by their No.

Despite these facts, God remains Yes to Israel. Our case with God is similar. God in Christ said Yes to us when we exited the bondage of Satan and sin by our call to repentance and our baptism in the waters of our salvation. Like the Israelites, we haven't kept a steady faith and love. We are offered the second exodus from the Babylon of our sins in the sacrament of penance.

Do we notice that God in Christ is saying Yes again to us? Do we celebrate the sacrament frequently as a response to God's exclamation in this reading: "See, I am doing something new!"?

Paul, in the second reading, answers the charge that he vacillates. He says that he has always tried to imitate Christ, that his response to the salvation and call of Christ has been a true and total Yes. Because Jesus' response to the Father was always Yes, I like to think not so much of written Scriptures as the one-word, living Scripture Who is Jesus. And I would like to kneel my head and my heart before this Scripture with all the Yes I can muster. With Paul, I affirm that Jesus is my true and sole Savior. He is man's greatest Yes to God, and I offer my Yes joined to His and to Him. Do you?

In the Gospel, the paralytic is healed by Jesus. Just as the Israelites had to be carried through the sea to freedom and wholeness, so the paralytic must pass "through a hole in the roof" into the healing and liberating presence of Jesus. There is a greater point to this story. Jesus uses this incident to claim the godly power of forgiving men's sins. The dramatic physical cure is but an external proof of the Lord's ability to forgive sin. The observant reader of the Bible will note that the very first gift-power Jesus gives the Apostles after His Resurrection is that of forgiving men their sins. "Whose sins you shall forgive, they are forgiven them!"

Saying Yes to God through His Christ is the theme of today's readings. God is always Yes to our needs. Like

Jesus, we must strive to be only Yes to the Father in our responses. In the sacrament of penance our Yes meets His. In every commandment we keep and in every deed of love we do, we are specifying and interpreting the one great Yes of our baptism unto salvation. We should see our religion this way. We should see all our fidelities this way. Our Yes to God in Christ must be allowed to filter down to familiar things in our lives—like wives in curlers, grubby kids, the retching sick, the wretched poor, the aging with their fears, and the aged with their immense vulnerability.

The Christian Yes to God covers an immense spread. We cannot allow it second place to the call of the consumer commercials and the Yes to Martini & Rossi on the rocks.

Cycle B   Eighth Sunday in Ordinary Time

MY FAITH AS MY MARRIAGE

Readings: *Hosea 2:16-17, 21-22; 2 Corinthians 3:1-6;*
        Mark 2:18-22

We tend to look at our beautiful Faith as a set of doctrines to which we give our assent. Or we see it as a code of morality to be inculcated and adhered to strictly. Our Faith is, indeed, not less than these factors—but it is also a lot more. It is a love story, the greatest love story ever told and acted out in human history.

Today's first reading is from Hosea, the prophet who first introduces the theology of religion as a love relationship with God. Hosea saw Israel as the bride of Yahweh, and the saving deeds of Yahweh toward Israel as so many moments and motions of tenderness.

Hosea's theology of religion as a marriage is based in two so-called "modern" ideas—existentialism and personalism. It is out of the experiences of his own love for his own faithless wife that Hosea builds his theological vision of Yahweh and Israel. It is out of his own tender and forgiving heart that he sees the heart of Yahweh as an endless reservoir of mercy and loving kindness. If man is the image of God, the heart of the husband Hosea is a true reflection of the heart of God.

The same idea of our faith life as a life of marriage with God is found in the second reading. Paul speaks of "a new covenant." It is not written in law as human contracts are written. It is written in the love that defines the Spirit of God. You and I are "covenanted" to God in Christ. We are "married" to Him.

In the Gospel, Jesus describes His relationship with the Apostles (and Church) not as law or religion but as love. "How can the guests at the wedding fast as long as the groom is still among them?"

Today, we might reflect on the import of our faith as a love relationship, a covenant of love, and a marriage with God in Christ. The TV commercial tells us to "put some life in your love and put some love in your life." We must expand our notion of religion beyond a set of doctrines and a code of laws. Faith is a life to be lived. It is a love life to be experienced, made happy through, and delighted in. It is a bonding or a wedding of hearts.

Paul mentions his preaching to and conversion of his converts as "a love letter" from God to them. Could we not read the many passages of Scripture as so many love letters from our loving God to us? Could we not approach prayer as heart-to-heart conversation with our Bridegroom and the several sacraments as so many embraces of love and healing? Could we not visit the Blessed Sacrament as the quiet, unspoken meeting point of two lovers who need neither gesture nor word in each other's presence? And could we not see—even feel—the ultimate level of loving presence and intimacy?

Paul says of his beloved (if erratic) Corinthians: "You are my letter . . . written on your hearts." Each of us should learn to see himself and herself as a love letter God has written. I am the incarnation of the love of His Heart, a very special kind of scripture. I am also His letter of love, kindness, forgiveness, and mercy to the world around me. I would do well to appreciate my religion as my marriage with God, His sacraments as so many loving encounters and embraces, my prayers as lovers' conversations, and my very self (however startling the fact) as His letter of love to others.

Cycle B   Ninth Sunday in Ordinary Time

HUMAN CONCERN COMES FIRST

Readings: *Deuteronomy 5:12–15; 2 Corinthians 4:6–11; Mark 2:23–3:6*

The shocking saga of the American hostages in Iran outraged the nation. Taking hostages (and treating them with abandon and even death) has become a common occurrence. We have known for centuries that life is cheap chattel in many lands. Human life is getting cheaper in the West as we pawn it for personal gain in kidnapping, exploitation, and abortion.

What is truly more alarming is the secularization of Western civilization, because human life, bereft of its theological definition, becomes more and more "disposable." Much of the opposition to an "easier" death is just a matter of law, not theology. We may expect a more "selective" and "limited" concern for human life at the beginning, middle, and terminal points in the immediate future based on our collapse into secularization.

Today's readings are a manifesto of Christian concern for human life, for the primacy of human life, and for the primacy of human concern. Jesus is Lord of the sabbath (Gospel) and superior to all law. He is also Lord of love, and He insists (through this Gospel) on our loving concern for fellow human beings. In the same way, the "sabbath" or "rest day" of the Lord (first reading) is a statement of human concern and human primacy over secular toil, ambitions, goals, and slavery. God's children come *before* man's concern for progress or exploitation of the earth.

In the second reading, Paul asks us to speak a "body language" that reveals the love and suffering of Jesus. He cannot become the Lord of our lives, as He is the Lord of the sabbath, without our acceptance of pain and a proper transfiguration of it in imitation of Him. In this way, He truly becomes our total Lord and the Lord of creation.

Today we are becoming more and more concerned (rightly) about the dismantling of law and the law's dismantling of traditional supports for religion, life, family life, virtues, and values. We are speaking of the secular or civil law. It has become oppressive to many of us, and to the kind of lordship we wish to promote and serve on this planet. In times past—and even yet today—another kind of legalism has tended to crush some and debase others in the name of religion, of Church, of Christ, and of His Lordship. We watch, with dismay, arrogance abroad in the Church in the matters of covert selection for leadership roles, lack of due process, reliance on expected "docility," imposition of new programs said to be based in doctrine or Vatican II, racism reflected in charges of racism, and talent left fallow for fear of competition. All of us are a long way from authentic human concern within the Church. We are, as yet, too concerned about our own traditions, skin color, theologies, and single-item passions.

Jesus said, "The sabbath was made for man, not man for the sabbath." He is also saying that the Church, and the law (anyone's law, including even God's), and leadership, and offices, and systems of dogma and morality are made to serve man. Man is not here to serve them. Let us adjust our thinking and our activity to human concern as the priority.

Cycle B   Tenth Sunday in Ordinary Time

THE SCANDAL OF TRUTH

Readings: *Genesis 3:9–15; 2 Corinthians 4:13–5:1; Mark 3:20–35*

Cardinal Danielou once wrote a book titled *The Scandal of Truth*. In the "Little Rules" which the seminarian Angelo Roncalli (Pope John XXIII) followed was an emphasis on knowing the truth about oneself, facing it, and correcting oneself according to it. Truth is hard to face, whether it pertains to oneself or others. We are embarrassed in confronting our weakness and jealous in facing the truth about others' fortune or fame in men's eyes.

Truth, however, is necessary and salutary. It builds the better person and the better earth. To avoid it is to—somehow—avoid the Holy Spirit of God, to promote personal fragmentation, and to war against the human family. Such seems to me the import of the readings today.

The first reading shows the "spiral" of relational collapse set in motion by the denial of truth. Adam blames Eve; she blames the serpent; they become divorced from garden and grace. Lie and denial originate with the serpent and at the beginning of the human odyssey so its import must be crucial to religion (i.e., relationship with God). Religious truth (or the truth that alone saves a man) is said to be in Christians as a "spirit of faith" (second reading). Its source is the Holy Spirit, Which attests to the saving truth of Jesus and His followers. We must speak this truth to ourselves and to our time. Else, we deny the Spirit. Am I speaking this saving truth of faith to myself, my behavior, my priorities, my family, my friends, my competitors, my enemies? Am I denying saving truth to my children in the matters of religious knowledge and church attendance? Are my priorities, ambitions, lifestyle, and values ordered under "the gaze of what is seen" rather than under "the gaze of what is unseen" (second reading)?

We are prone to oppose truth at every level of life. And when the truth is too telling or too demanding we profess the purest of innocence or the vilest antipathy. Faced with the power of truth in Jesus and the attraction of their people to Him, ". . . scribes who arrived from Jerusalem asserted 'He is possessed by the Devil . . . He expels demons with the help of the prince of demons.'" Even "His family," beset by embarrassment and poor perception, protested, "He is out of His mind!"

When we are confronted with a truth about ourselves that evokes the response "You're out of your mind," it is possible that this is the one truth most necessary for us to hear. Hear it! It will be a saving truth.

The truth of Jesus is the truth of God. It is the truth that saves, and it is final truth. We must accept it, believe on it, and act on it. Not to do so is to deny the Spirit.

Cycle B   Eleventh Sunday in Ordinary Time

A THEOLOGY OF SMALLNESS

Readings: *Ezekiel 17:22-24; 2 Corinthians 5:6-10; Mark 4:26-34*

"Big gifts sometimes come in small parcels." So goes the saying. It is spoken to console the small of stature or to assure the Martys and the Fatsos of our culture that women can also fall for men who are not "tall, dark, and handsome."

It would seem that Jesus is answering the critics of His "kingdom" in today's Gospel. Some there were who felt that an inauspicious rabbi from the God-forsaken village of Bethlehem was no incarnation of a king in David's line. And was a band of the lower class (called Apostles) a worthy base on which to rebuild the kingdom of Israel—and to its messianic proportions at that?

Our Lord seems to answer His critics in the two parables of today's Gospel. In the first parable, He implies that the Kingdom of God (in Him) grows imperceptibly by God's command and gift. In the second parable, He notes how small the mustard seed is, yet how large the tree that grows from it. Here and in the first reading there is mention of "birds of every kind" being sustained by this tree. God's Kingdom, initiated by Jesus and offered to all by the Apostles, shall be a Kingdom greater than David's, greater than the expected restoration, great enough for all Jews and all Gentiles as well!

Let us be consoled in that no matter how small we perceive ourselves to be, God in Christ has made us part of this Kingdom of love, peace, and justice. It does not really matter that we are the "small people" of "this passing age" in terms of wealth, power, influence, and prestige. It *does* really matter that we, not the sleek of society, have been chosen and called to the Kingdom that counts.

Let us defer to the Good Lord Who chose us and elected us without merit or power of our own; Who makes us to grow in His favor and grace before Him like the insignificant seed; Who has "disinherited the mighty" by giving us greatness through a theology of smallness. It is the amazing grace of our Christian God that power is eternally insignificant and weakness is always full of significance.

Let us take some personal pains to give gift for gift, to offer our significant "insignificance" by word and witness to others that they, too, might come to the Kingdom that counts so that "birds of all kinds" shall inherit it and inhabit it. The final number in the

Kingdom ("Are they few, Lord, who are to be saved?") is known only to God. We should not assume it will be a small number. If anything, the seed that mushroomed and the smallness that is so significant are imperatives that, by word and witness, we invite *all* in our ambit to the Kingdom that counts.

Cycle B   Twelfth Sunday in Ordinary Time

RISKING IT WITH JESUS

Readings: *Job 38:1, 8-11; 2 Corinthians 5:14-17; Mark 4:35-41*

We are familiar with the advertising that stresses the comparative lack of risk if we save with, insure with, or invest with X or Y company. The face for this little-risk firm is always quietly studious, touched with the slightest silver, and backdropped in mahogany. He (not my fault, ladies) has the calm of Jesus (without the fishing boat). The building he inhabits is among the tallest, safest, most substantial, and most secure in the city. It is saying to you: "Invest with me—at little risk."

Much is made of the high risk we adopt with Jesus. It is my belief that such a view is based in little faith. If anything, the image of a sleeping Jesus in the bow of a small boat amid perilous waves is a reassurance of safe passage, not risk, with Him. Contrasted here are the power of the waves and the calm of Jesus; the fear of experienced fishermen and the inner peace of Jesus; the might of the elements and the mightier power of Jesus; the risk of faith in a boat and the absence of risk in the arm of God. "Why are you afraid? Why are you so lacking in faith?" There is no risk for those with faith in

One Whose power is cosmic in scope (Gospel)! Who else on this planet can assure our investment in him as this One Whom "the wind and the sea obey"? In another place, He said, "All power is given to Me in heaven and on earth!" We risk nothing with Him!

Jesus, now reigning in glory, is Lord of the cosmos, of life, of history. In Him the words of Job (first reading) are fulfilled: "here shall your proud waves be stilled."

He is Lord of creation too, and more especially of spiritual creation. In Him, and through the "risk" we have taken with Him, we have become "a new creation" (second reading). On all levels, "the old order has passed away; now all is new."

These Scriptures (in particular, Mark's Gospel passage) are offered the early Church (and ourselves) as a theology of hope, assurance, and confidence. They are insisting on the "no-risk policy" that Jesus offers, having shown us His Lordship over diseases and elements and every factor the human mind, body, and soul must contend with in their natural passage or pilgrimage of faith.

It is for us now, as single believers and Church community, to respond with faith and confidence. God in Christ watches over us with power as well as concern. We must put our problems and our passages into His hands. No force can destroy us in any significant way, and the most salutary responses are made by His care to fit our needs.

Risking it with Jesus is no risk for the believer. It is the sure investment of time and life with One Whose policy is utterly benign and utterly fail-safe.

Cycle B   Thirteenth Sunday in Ordinary Time

DEATH AS MY PASSOVER

Readings: *Wisdom 1:13–15, 2:23–24; 2 Corinthians 8:7, 9, 13–15;
Mark 5:21–43*

Most of us are ambivalent about death. We're not too
sure about how to face it or what attitude a Christian
should have toward it. Some feel that death is a reaper
cutting down life ruthlessly. Others see death as the
great release from a stupid and madding world. The
depressed are like the poet "half in love with easeful
death."

The Bible yields many attitudes toward death because
it is the reflection of man's ambivalence as well as the inspired word of God. However, the readings in this Sunday's Mass teach us some basic attitudes in the theology
of death.

"God did not make death" and "God formed man to
be imperishable," we are told in the first reading. Where
did death come from, then? It came from "the envy of
the Devil." We recall that it was the serpent who tempted
our first parents to sin and, as St. Paul says, "with sin,
death entered the world." We must be very careful,
then, about attributing death and destruction to the will
of God. A President is assassinated and we say it's the
will of God. A child is killed by a drunk driver and we
call that the will of God too. Death and human destruction come from Satan and sin: they do not come from
God. The second reading suggests that all human
"want"—poverty, inequality, injustice—results from
forms of death and becomes forms of death. We are

asked to share our abundance with others as a counter-sign and counteraction to death.

These readings affirm life and condemn death in its spiritual and material forms.

The theme is continued by Jesus in the Gospel. Here, He heals the hemorrhaging woman (partial death) and raises to life the little dead girl of twelve (full death). He, the Author of Life, is Himself the great Counter-sign of death. He works mightily against death in all its forms because they all flow from sin. We can work mightily against sin—death forms—in ourselves, in our neighbors, in our neighborhoods.

The basic Christian approach to our personal death "in the flesh" has to be that of Our Lord. We shall triumph over death like Him, passing through the veil of time and limitation and service into the eternity of life. We should regard our whole life span on earth as our Passover, with physical death as the climax. We are moving, in the continuum of the Servant of God, from limitation to liberation. Israel of old went through this Passover. So did the patriarchs and prophets of faith. So did Jesus. So must we.

"I am going the way of all flesh" need not be a lamentation. As Christ-followers, we are going on our personal passovers from shadow to substance; from fragmentary life to wholeness of living; from long-held hope to realization. Believers should always remind themselves that the sacraments are signs and energies of the new life leading to full communion with God. Even as we decline "in the flesh," we are being raised from sin's deadly condition.

Cycle B   Fourteenth Sunday in Ordinary Time

INDEPENDENCE: WHAT FOR?

Readings: *Ezechiel 2:2–5; 2 Corinthians 12:7–10; Mark 6:1–6*

The Scripture readings of the Mass of the Fourteenth Sunday, by happy coincidence, bear on the independence theme of July 4th, our national holiday which falls about this time. We celebrate political freedom. These readings speak of the tragedy of closing ourselves into old and hardened ways while resisting the new word, the new idea, and the new day. Israel resisted the prophets sent to her by God. She also resisted the new life, the new day, and the new Word, Jesus.

Somewhere I have read that in 1776 about a third of the colonial populace resisted independence; another third couldn't have cared less; but, fortunately, a third promoted the new idea, the new life, and the new day. Whence, America!

Both experiences, Christian and American, speak to us with a kind of shock. They tell us how easily many people are prepared to remain in the old, familiar slaveries and not risk a better way. They show how a few prophets or a single Savior are put upon by the very people they suffer and die to save. Independence is dearly won and dearly maintained. We humans don't always appreciate a good thing when it is fashioned for us. Even in our liberation we still hanker after the irresponsibility of old fleshpots and the security of predetermined slaveries. They are "the filthy but familiar dust."

Today is a day for rejoicing. Let us, therefore, be glad and exult in it! Thank God for a free land, our freedom in Christ, and our grace to pursue both future and destiny.

But perhaps America is cresting with this Bicentennial. The open and inevitable material progress is suddenly conditioned. The waste and surplus that had no end now is limited. The small people are unemployed, undervisioned, and aggravated by the millions. The big people are caught by their capers in the thousands. The spiritual dynamic—the nation's original primer—is bent with every poll. Proportionately inactive is the persuasive power of fifty million Catholics.

I wish these Catholics one blessing on July 4th: that they rise from the seat of their apathy and let their voice be heard on the issues shaping this land. They are clobbered year after year by the forces of secularization, and they take it like a preordained malediction of Fate. They have bought the charge that activity on their part would be the imposition of sectarian morality on the nation. As if the nation would allow this, and as if the other forces were not imposing their codes on the body politic!

Let us worry instead about our silence and others' activity. Worry about the power and the efficiency of the controlling elements who were once ignoble to our forefathers and marginal to the health of the nation: the criminals, the underground subversives, the secular humanists, the pornographers, the abortionists, the home wreckers, and the seditionists against a civilized society. Bless them at least for their determination: they have spoken well and effectively in the absence of fifty million American Catholics.

Cycle B   Fifteenth Sunday in Ordinary Time

TO TELL THE WORLD

Readings: *Amos 7:12–15; Ephesians 1:3–14; Mark 6:7–13*

The theme of this Sunday's readings at Mass is the disciples' commission to share and extend the message and the saving grace of the Gospel. In other words, part of our calling in Christ is to "win souls for him" and gather them into the fellowship of His Church, which is the visible and social dimension of the Kingdom of God on earth.

Contemporary Catholics, in the aftermath of Vatican II and all its traumatic reorientations, are among the most inactive of American Christians as far as domestic evangelization is concerned. We don't seem to have the old zeal for convert making or a clear realization that ecumenism does not excuse us from encouraging others to the fullness of truth and life that mark the Church of Peter. It was the Lord's intention that we have truth and life "to the full."

Let us have the vision of our missionary calling even if, like Amos, the world or the image makers say to us, "Off with you, visionary!" Let us keep insisting on the inner connection between evangelization and Church membership (see Acts) even in the company of theological sophists. Let us be clear that the "social gospel" is integral to the missionary mandate, but it is not coextensive with or a replacement for the preaching of the blood of Christ "through which we have been redeemed and our sins forgiven." Let us not democratize our commission into a "live and let live" excuse: after all, to try to "sell" a product that really saves people is in the best American tradition! We are not called to coerce others but to persuade them. When our invitation is rejected, it is quite all right "to shake the dust from your feet" and move on. Just be sure your word and your witness are full of the persuasive grace and power of the Lord and not blocked by your own shrill conceits and condemnations.

No doubt we all stand in need of reevangelization even if we are priests and deacons and bishops and secular saints. Like Israel of old, we are chosen and gathered yet spend forty years wandering in the Wilderness of Sin, the wildernesses of our own weaknesses and failures. We may have wandered far from "our first love," forgetting that in Jesus we were chosen and redeemed and made God's adopted sons and daughters. Such was "God's will and pleasure" toward us.

Charity begins at home and spreads out from us to others. We may say the same this Sunday of our calling in Christ and of our commission to spread the Good News of salvation. We cannot be disciples without taking the call to our hearts and the commission to others.

Cycle B   Sixteenth Sunday in Ordinary Time

SHEPHERDING THE '80s

Readings: *Jeremiah 23:1–6; Ephesians 2:13–18; Mark 6:30–34*

Preachers have a penchant for texts beginning with "Woe!" So the first line of this Sunday's readings at Mass may well be the sermon line of diatribes against theologians and bishops across the land. "Woe to the shepherds who mislead and scatter the flock of my pasture, says the Lord." Homilists should resist the temptation: it only contributes to raising the "barriers of hostility" and to destroying "the good news of peace" which are the subject of the second reading.

Better, instead, that each priest and each Christian at Mass this Sunday reach into his secret heart and discover how he is shepherding his parish, his family, his employees, his concerns and ambitions along the way of the Kingdom and in the prescribed areas of "unity" and "peace." Even more to the point is not our shepherding of others but our docility to the word, the grace, and the presence of Christ, the model Shepherd.

I don't believe there is a shepherd—ordained or lay—of any consequence to the Kingdom who is not allowing himself to be led "in the Spirit to the Father." You cannot lead in the Kingdom without being led yourself by the Spirit. One wonders why so little seems to result from bishops' meetings, priests' councils, and lay groups. Perhaps it has to do with the furtive opening prayer, the automatically built-in "slot" for the Liturgy. Added up, these holy gestures do not outrank the time given to social hours and dinners.

We note that Jesus and the Apostles, as shepherds in the Gospel reading, had to withdraw and rest awhile from sheer exhaustion because "people were coming and going in great numbers, making it impossible for them to so much as eat." Yet even here there was no rest because "many got to know about it, arriving at the rest-place ahead of them." Our Lord did not throw up His hands at "the tyranny of the people" but pitied them "for they were like sheep without a shepherd." And "he began to teach them—at great length."

The shepherd must be clear on "the teaching." It is the Good News of unity and peace and salvation made present through the blood of Christ. He must be led by the Spirit of God if he is to lead others. This calls for the discernment that comes from study, strategy, prayer, and fasting. Accountability is to the Spirit and to one's own sense of compassion. Conditions are not dependent on faculties, unions, and regulations but on the need and press of the people.

It's a hard line, this business of shepherding your parish or your own family or your own individual spirit. It is even more complex in the 1980s. But the bottom line on it is the Spirit. Only those led by the Spirit can shepherd because only "those led by the Spirit of God are the sons of God."

Cycle B   Seventeenth Sunday in Ordinary Time

THE GOD OF PLENTY

Readings: *2 Kings 4:42–44; Ephesians 4:1–6; John 6:1–15*

We have long been accused by Communists and other hard-nosed social theorists of diverting the poor's attention from present hunger by promising them "a pie in the sky when you die." If this is true, then religion is just "the opium of the poor people." It distracts them from the hunger pains in their stomachs, from the hopelessness of their poverty, and it concentrates their last energies on the hope of a Heaven beyond space and time.

That summary is not accurate. However, we may be accused now and then of overly concentrating on the afterlife to the detriment of pressing social inequalities and injustices. The truth of Scripture is that the believer is called to restore this present earth to its original justice and goodness, while at the same time remembering "we have not here a lasting city but seek one yet to come." We Christians are committed to justice, peace, and plenty in the temporal order *and* to the everlasting glory of the afterlife. The one is expressed in our dedication to the "social gospel" of Isaiah's messianic vision, the other is expressed in our hard pursuit of the beatific vision or the heavenly Jerusalem. There need be no conflict between the two.

Elisha's miraculous multiplication of the bread (first reading) foreshadows our Lord's miracle of multiplication (third reading). Paul urges us (second reading) to a multiplication or plentifulness of virtue, which reflects the plenitude of God who is "Father of all, who is over all, and works through all, and is in all." Whether we are speaking of this world or the next, our God is the God of plenty Who provides abundantly for His children in the matter of bread, or healing, or grace, or virtue. Many symbols express this abundance of God. We think of the cornucopia (the horn of plenty) in the Old Testament and the heavenly banquet of the Kingdom parables in the New Testament.

For St. John, Jesus is the new and greater Moses who feeds God's children with the plentifulness of the Eucharist just as Moses fed the children of Israel in the wilderness of sin with the manna from Heaven. But there is a great difference. "Your fathers ate the manna in the desert but [eventually] died. The bread that I will give is my flesh for the life of the world . . . He who eats my flesh and drinks my blood has everlasting life and I will raise him up on the last day."

We are dealing with three kinds of bread and hunger in today's readings. There are the bread of the stomach, the bread of moral virtue and witness, and the bread of the Eucharist. Each bread, in turn, points us beyond itself to the everlasting banquet with Christ which we call Heaven. This is, of course, "the ultimate hope of your calling."

Let us commit ourselves to alleviating the hungers of the human family through the bread of justice and sharing. Let us break the bread of moral virtue with all who enter our sphere of influence. Let us feast regularly at the Lord's table of Eucharist. And let each of these forms of bread point us and power us to its own ultimate symbolization—the hope that one day we will sit down in glory with Christ at His Father's heavenly banquet that has no end of joy and plenty.

Cycle B   Eighteenth Sunday in Ordinary Time

TRUTH AS BREAD

Readings: *Exodus 16:2–4, 12–15; Ephesians 4:17, 20–24;*
          John 6:24–35

Down through the centuries the character, life, and words of St. Francis of Assisi have touched minds and hearts of all kinds. Believers and agnostics alike have been entranced by St. Francis. The pious associate him with the crib of Christmas. The ecologists love him for his regard of the environment. The animal lovers cherish him for his dialogic approach to animals. All of us yearn for a measure of his simplicity. Few of us, perhaps, are aware of the fact that Francis's great love was the Eucharist.

Today's readings anticipate Jesus as our Eucharist as they bear first upon Him as the "bread of truth."

In the first reading, we recall the feeding of our Israelite forefathers with manna from Heaven during their pilgrimage from bondage to liberation. In the second reading, Paul reminds us that we Christians have been fed with another manna, the truth of Jesus. In the Gospel reading, Jesus reminds us to desire this bread of truth. "You should not be striving for perishable bread but for bread which remains unto life eternal."

What is the truth Jesus calls bread unto eternal life? It is not scientific truth. It is not economic truth. It is not philosophical truth. It is not any form of human wisdom or technological expertise. It is *saving* truth. It is the only truth that ultimately saves a human being. The saving truth is Jesus. In Him we become the adopted sons and daughters of God. A number of pastoral points flow from this. There are many valid "truths" of value but only one saving Truth. The Truth which makes us free and feeds our aspiration toward eternal life ought to top our list of important truths. I do not say that we should ignore other truths. We can pursue beauty as truth, science as truth, patriotism as truth. Just let saving truth be the all-important and ceaseless pursuit.

On the other hand, let us not be listed among the growing numbers of antiintellectual Christians who confuse the saving Truth of Jesus with all truth possible in the universe. These rigid Bible toters, a plague to both

Church and intellectual life, would shut down all scholarship and all scientific endeavor and all speculation if they had their way. They restrict the mercy of God and the profuse blood of the Savior to their own taut mentality.

You may note how the airwaves are polluted presently with another Bible-toting, truth-constricting lot—the fundamentalists and the apocalyptic interpreters. The former reduce the inspired word of God to a literalness which makes mockery of man's intelligence. Are any of us supporting these self-appointed teachers? The latter (always popular with the ignorant and the fearful) interpret Joel and Daniel and John as though these spiritual giants were merely visionary experts in oil, multinational corporations, modern military assignments, and Middle East politics. I'm quite sure that John, as an old man, did not stand on Patmos nineteen hundred years ago dictating his Apocalypse as a tract on 1980 Russian strategy in the Mediterranean. Yet this is television Christianity in Los Angeles: junk food for bread.

Last, in our culture of secularization, let us pay heed to St. Paul. We are not to "swing" like the pagans—"their minds empty." We are, instead, to come under the moral truth of Jesus. We must "lay aside the former way of living and the old self which deteriorates through illusion and desire." What about all our sex, drugs, booze, violence, lies, cheating, and lack of concern? Rather, "you must put on the new man created in God's image, whose rightness and justice and holiness are born of truth."

Cycle B   Nineteenth Sunday in Ordinary Time

BREAD FOR THE JOURNEY

Readings: *1 Kings 19:4–8; Ephesians 4:30–5:2; John 6:41–51*

We are familiar with the description of man's life on earth as a journey. Man himself is a *viator*, one walking down the road of life's years. Where is he going? It's a simple question. It's also one of the two or three greatest philosophical questions. Who am I? Where have I come from? Where am I going?

The first reading this Sunday answers the great question. I am like the prophet Elijah "on a journey through the desert . . . to the mountain of the Lord." My present life is only a pilgrimage. I am passing through, bent on Mount Zion, the heavenly Jerusalem, the beatific vision, the permanent rapture of God's presence and love. I am on this journey. You are on this journey. Both of us, as Church, are on the journey. "We have not here a lasting city but are seeking one yet to be."

How are we to conduct ourselves as we pass along in our pilgrimage? Paul, in the second reading, gives some answers. We are to "follow the way of love, even as Christ loved you." He lists some of the specifications of the way of love: no bitterness over disappointments; no irrational passion and anger; no harsh words to those who destroy our confidence, our hope, and our health; malice toward none. We are all God's children, and there is only a difference in degree between our common sins. Be kind, compassionate, and forgiving. Why? Not just for heroics but because Christ has already offered us to His Father as "a gift of pleasing fragrance."

Does Christ sustain us on our journey as the Lord Yahweh sustained Elijah with food on his? He does. In the third reading, we learn about this sustaining food. It is the Bread of Life. This Bread of Life has two forms. It is the saving Word of God and it is the Body and Blood of Jesus as our Eucharist. It is the spiritual bread of truth and the literal flesh of the Savior. We need both on our way.

Jesus speaks about both kinds of bread in the third reading. First, he speaks of His teaching: "It is written in the prophets 'they shall be taught by God.' Everyone who has heard the Father and learned from him comes to me." Jesus, the Teacher, is our spiritual bread. Eating this bread is the symbol (taken from Old Testament Wisdom Literature) for our hearing and receiving the saving Word of God. Next, Jesus speaks of Himself as bread in another sense. "The bread I *will* give is my *flesh* for the life of the world." The structure of the Mass actually patterns the move of the Gospel passage from one bread to the other. We have, first, the liturgy of the word, then, the liturgy of Eucharist.

One thing remains—our faith response. The effectiveness of both breads rests with our faith. "Let me firmly assure you, he who believes has eternal life." The Word of God was not intended to go forth among men and return empty. The Eucharist is not broken by Jesus among empty hearts and absent families. We, at least, have heard and believe. We believe and, therefore, we accept the saving Word and eat the consecrated Bread. We welcome the Lord on our journey and are fed by Him through His Scripture and His sacrament. Yet we yearn for Him even beyond them. Come, Lord, quickly and finally to meet us out of the future even as we journey in faith to Your mountain!

Cycle B   Twentieth Sunday in Ordinary Time

THE BREAD OF ETERNAL LIFE

Readings: *Proverbs 9:1-6; Ephesians 5:15-20; John 6:51-58*

Just the other day a parishioner called me by phone. "I've been listening to you at Mass and I want to talk to you. I have a problem keeping the Church with God in my life." I checked her census file and felt I knew what the topic of our appointment would be. At age 29, with four young children, a new job, and a touch of anxiety in the voice, the issue might be birth control. It was.

Let me leave the issue there. The point at issue here is the way we develop "problems" and "crises of conscience" with the Church or with doctrine as soon as they begin to impinge with some pain on our lives, styles, beliefs, and behaviors. To borrow the movie title, we start "breaking away" when the Cross enters our lives. But we do not do it cleanly. We put the finger on someone else as though he (or she or it) had created our newfound problem for us. To make matters worse, we drive a neat wedge between God (Who, of course, always remains on *our* side) and that other person, Church, or law that has become the enemy in our religious life.

Youngsters, too, in our time have developed a huge "problem" with the Church in the matter of their relationship with Jesus. It is highlighted in the issue of Sunday Mass or Eucharist. For their instruction, we should attend closely to the Scriptures of Jesus in today's readings. It is He Who commands Eucharist, not the Church or the Pope or any institution divorced from Him. It is He Who met angry opposition from the ordinary people on the issue of Eucharist and He Who found even His disciples breaking away "and walking no more with Him."

Wisdom (first reading) invites all to "come and eat" at her table of plenty in her temple of "understanding." Leave aside your confusion and enter this temple of God for "understanding." It is John (today's Gospel author) who takes wisdom to mean the Word of God (Jesus) in all its truth and fullness. Jesus is "the wisdom of God."

In the Gospel, Wisdom offers Himself to the believer as the most intimate and sustaining life possible for this life and the next. He offers this wisdom as moral truth, as saving truth, in the form of His preaching and commandments and *now*—in its greatest form—as the Eucharist of love and life.

"Unless you eat of the flesh of the Son of Man and drink His blood, you have no life in you. . . . He who feeds on my flesh and drinks my blood has life eternal, and I will raise him up on the last day!" It is Jesus—not the Church—Who says that without Eucharist "you have *no life* in you." And at the Final Supper with His closest friends, it was He—not the Church—Who commanded them: "Do *this* in remembrance of Me."

Nowhere does Jesus "command" private prayer on sabbath or Sunday, or communal prayer on any beach in preference to the reenactment of His Last Supper. It is *this* He has commanded, as the measure of love and life. If we have a "problem" with It, we have a "problem" not with the Church but with Him. Let us be honest when pointing fingers.

Cycle B   Twenty-first Sunday in Ordinary Time

FAITH: AN UNCALCULATED RISK

Readings: *Josua 24:1-2, 15-17, 18; Ephesians 5:21-32; John 6:60-69*

We pride ourselves on our ability to analyze a situation and calculate a risk. That is prudent. It is also good economics. It works well in all the practical areas of life. So we try to apply it to faith, morals, and love as well. That is a mistake. Calculation and analysis have no place in the affairs of the heart. You cannot analyze the chemistry of love. You cannot calculate the risk of love.

Religion, at root, is a love relationship between the human heart and the heart of God. The Bible calls it a marriage. You cannot plan or plot the marriage process—only the initial ceremony. We agree to risk the marriage with God. Faith is then a risk. He asks for our hand and our trust. As the years unfold, He does not always tell us that He is walking hand-in-hand with us, nor does He always give clear touches of His abiding presence. Like the Israelites of the first reading, the heart alone senses He is with us, continues to speak to us, and has been holding our hand firmly all the time, even in the deepest depressions and the darkest of nights. At Shechem in the full light of freedom, Israel renewed her covenanted love with Yahweh. In the brightness of the Sunday Eucharist, the Church renews Her covenanted love with the Lord.

St. Paul, in the second reading, continues to speak of our covenanted love as a marriage. He uses the marriage relationship of humans to illustrate the union of hearts that is brought about by my faith commitment with God and the Church's faith commitment with Christ. "The two become one." The risk has to be total to be anything at all.

In the Gospel reading, we have the conclusion of our Lord's discourse on the Bread of Life. He has spoken of Himself as the Bread of Life in several senses. Here, He forewarns that the risk of faith is needed to accept the Eucharist as His literal flesh and blood. Only those who love Him utterly can accept such teaching. His hearers "murmur among themselves." They argue and reason when they should have simply risked their love. And so "many of his disciples broke away and walked no more with him."

Yes, faith in and love of God are a risk. They don't do very well in the analytical and calculating mind. But, then, it's not a matter of the mind but an issue of the heart. You can give "reasons" why you believe in your spouse, your children, your country, and your close friends. But you cannot give compelling reasons because you know all too well that they—like everyone else—have feet of clay and a bundle of blemishes. You still believe in them because the heart has totally committed itself almost without your knowing.

It is the same with our risk of faith. Despite all the darkness and the contradictions, I know God has invaded my heart and I have responded. I am married to Him despite my failings, and I would not have it any other way. It all comes down to a loving faith in which the heart speaks its own reasons in its own language to Him rather than to me. "Jesus then said to the Twelve, 'Will you also leave me?' Simon Peter answered him, 'Lord, to whom shall we go? Your words are words of eternal life; and we have come to believe that you are God's holy one.'"

Cycle B   Twenty-second Sunday in Ordinary Time

GETTING IN GOD'S WAY

Readings: *Deuteronomy 4:1-2, 6-8; James 1:17-18, 21-22, 27; Mark 7:1-8, 14-15, 21-23*

All of us have the tendency to clutter the saving word of God with our personal anxieties and private interpretations. This is often called "the human element" in religion. On a radio talk show last Sunday night, a Church of Christ minister set out to prove that his church was the true Church because the phrase "churches of Christ" appears in the Book of Revelation whereas there is no reference in the New Testament to a "Catholic Church," or to a "Lutheran Church," or to any other denomination!

We clutter up the saving word by our selection of texts that please us while by passing those that displease us. We spend a lot of time using (abusing is more like it) the Scriptures to "prove" this thing and that thing. The New Testament was not written as a debater's manual but as a simple record of the life of Jesus and the faith of the early Christian community in Him. He is the saving Word. We are not saved by a book—not even the Bible—but by the blood of Christ.

In the same way, the Church becomes cluttered with "the baggage of time." Pious practices tend to assume high places. Powerful personalities gain control of appointments (for example, in Iron Curtain countries). Institutionalization is always present. Laxity in morals and impurities in the Faith always threaten. The function of the Church's councils (such as Vatican II) is to renew the Church's spirit. She is always struggling to be the City on the mountaintop, the Bride adorned for her husband, the Light unto the illumination of the nations.

You and I should try to assist the Church in her great mission by keeping our "baggage" out of the way. We should not obscure the will of God by imposing contrary spirits, practices, and human foibles on it. Take to heart the warning of Yahweh to Israel in the first reading: "You shall not add to what I command you nor subtract from it." It was a warning ignored by the Pharisees of our Lord's time; it is a warning ignored by extremists of both sides in the Church today.

In the second reading, James—a letter, by the way, ignored and denied by some Christians—asks us to accept the word of God. Of course we accept it, we say! But do we accept it in its intrinsic freedom, or do we accept it on our terms only? The saving word must be received. It must be received humbly. And it must be acted upon, not just listened to. Those three conditions are most important. Do they represent the manner of our acceptance of the word?

In the Gospel reading, Jesus continues one of the greatest themes of His ministry, the liberation of the word and will of His Father from the interpretations and traditions of "religious" and "pious" men. We know well that He is the Savior of sinful men from their sins. But do we realize that He had to be the Savior of the word and will of God from the interpretations and theologies of fairly decent and holy men as well? That is a rather shocking fact. And what does it say to you and to me?

The reaction of saintly men and women to this has been a simple one. They have striven all the more to be simple and trusting like a child in its Father's house; to be fashioned by the will of the Father; to be pliable before His word; to listen well and act accordingly. "Nothing that enters a man from outside can make him impure. That which comes out of him—and only that—constitutes the impurity of religion." If an abundance of good works does not come out of us, an abundance of evil, debate, contention, private religion, and triviality will.

Cycle B   Twenty-third Sunday in Ordinary Time

WHO ARE THE POOR?

Readings: *Isaiah 35:4-7; James 2:1-5; Mark 7:31-37*

Jesus once said: "The poor you shall have with you always." How true! In an age of progress and how-to, we seem to have the poor and poverty in unparalleled proportions. We have differing reactions to the poor and to poverty. It is not a condition to be desired. Our Lord's remark should not be taken as a fatalistic projection of poverty. The first reading, in fact, heralds the abolition of poverty through the advent of the justice of the Messiah.

Biblical poverty is not defined in terms of economics alone. The leper is among the poor. So are the blind, the deaf, the maimed, the widow, and the orphan. Old Testament poverty is seen as the consequence of sin. So it is—but not as the measure of the afflicted's personal sin. It is the result of our corporate greed, unconcern, and selfishness. As we spread the Messiah's Kingdom across the earth (and through our own hearts), poverty is being abolished in all its forms.

St. James, in the second reading, contrasts poverty and pomp. At our table, we tend to sit the "man of substance" on our right while telling the poor man to "sit on the floor." How blind we are, says St. James. The well-off are not the subject of any of Jesus' promises, whereas the poor are promised a richness of faith and a claim to the Kingdom. Here is food for thought. The poor, the blind, the maimed, those alone may be more attuned to the Kingdom (because of their poverty) than the bothered if well-heeled rich. Our Lord did not condemn riches but He did point out their dangers. Riches simply add a further burden and a greater accountability to the Christian.

In the Gospel, Jesus heals the deaf man. "Ephphatha —be opened." As with His other miracles, this is not so much a work done as an end in itself but a work done as a sign that "the kingdom of God is in your midst."

Many lessons can be drawn from today's readings. For one thing, we Christians must be committed to the abolition of poverty because the Kingdom is already here. For another, we should give credit to the goodwill and technology that assist this work. Then we might ask ourselves whether, in a spirit contrary to St. James, we are given to the pomp bit—looking for kudos and honors even in the household of the faith. ("The kingdom of God does not come amid noise and fanfare.")

But, basic to all, we must come to grips with the spiritual meaning of these Scriptures on poverty. Who is really the poor man of the New Testament? Is it the physically maimed? Jesus said, "It is better for you to enter life maimed than to be cast into Gehanna whole." The Psalmist spoke for God: "They have eyes but see not; they have ears but hear not." Jesus said, "What does it profit a man to be rich with the whole world yet suffer the loss of his soul?" Clearly, physical poverty is an affliction but spiritual poverty is a calamity.

Let us renew our minds with the instructions of the Scripture, and redeem our hearts from our sins in the sacrament of penance. Until we do, *we* are poor, indeed.

Cycle B   Twenty-fourth Sunday in Ordinary Time

LOSE ALL: WIN ALL

Readings: *Isaiah 50:4-9; James 2:14-18; Mark 8:27-35*

There have always been men and women who felt that wealth and health are signs of God's favor while poverty and suffering are signs of His displeasure. God is said to bless His chosen ones with the horn of plenty and give them the land flowing with the milk and honey of material abundance. Nations have built empires on the premise that they were a chosen people and that the best of the earth was their title and patrimony.

This belief has given rise to concentration camps and confiscation policies, to servitude and slavery. We should be wary of "lording it over others," as Jesus said. How true to the mark He was when He said, "The one among you who would be greatest, let him be the servant of all." In the early books of the Old Testament there is a fairly consistent assumption that health is a sign of God's favor while suffering is a sign of His displeasure. Jesus would have none of this. He came out of the tradition of Isaiah who saw God's Messiah as a servant and as a suffering servant.

In the first reading today, we have one of the "songs of the Servant." It does not teach that suffering is in itself desirable but that it can be a sign of God's favor and presence. "He is near who upholds my right." The Psalmist had written earlier, "The Lord is near to the brokenhearted; close to those who are crushed in spirit."

James, in the second reading, teaches that faith without good works is dead. It should be understood from both Isaiah and Jesus that good works are not always the things we do. They are often the things we endure. The endurance of suffering is a salutary good work. Seeing it in this light, we may be better able to understand and to carry our broken dreams and broken hopes and broken persons. Nothing is totally lost, and nearly everything can be turned to gain for the man or woman who has put on the discipleship of the Servant.

We find, in the Gospel reading, that Peter is still back in the theology of the early Old Testament books. He is still the child of the health-and-wealth-and-power mentality. Not for him a Messiah who speaks of suffering, rejection, and death! Peter wants a glorious messianic kingdom of milk and honey right now—with himself as favorite son on the Master's footrest. The mother of Zebedee's sons wanted the same kind of kingdom, with her boys seated on the left and the right of the throne. Jesus said to her, "You do not know what you are asking." To Peter He said, "Get out of my sight, you satan! You are not judging by God's standards but by man's."

The true disciple must be ready to encounter suffering like everyone else. What he does with it is the all-important factor. It is not enough to put up with it. He must grow with it and through it in imitation of the Lord. Our suffering is our Cross, that accumulation of all the trials that beset us on our earthly pilgrimage.

Does each of us have, in addition, a "special" cross to bear? I believe so. This is the cross that really hurts, that weighs on the most vulnerable part of me. It is often my predominant weakness. It may be a shame or a disgrace that is public; it may be a depression or addiction that forever threatens; it may be the nights of despair or the years of loneliness. Strange as it may seem, the cross may be even one's docility to the word of God, the authority of the Church, or the quest for sanctity. They are countersigns to our age and we can be despised by friend as well as foe for such docility.

Whatever it is, I will find this cross at my very center—where I am most me. Perhaps this is why Jesus said that we must deny our very self. The self is a lot to lose. In fact, it is everything. But that's the way and the standard of the Servant who walked this way before us. "He who would save his life will lose it, but whoever loses his life for my sake and the Gospel's will save it."

NUMBER ONE IN GOD'S POLL

Readings: *Wisdom 2:12, 17–20; James 3:16–4:3; Mark 9:30–37*

The new college football season is here. Already the polls are projecting the bowl match-ups and the mythical national title. Who will be number one?

We take pride in this number one business. It's something of a national scandal. We just have to be the biggest and the best in everything, not merely in a mythical sport title. We think, like our New England ancestors, that God smiles on success. The past decade of chastisement should teach us that the biggest and the best systems in Church and state are no mark of God's favor. Both institutions are back in their locker rooms looking for their proper identities.

On the personal level we use up our energies—and often our principles—to come out on top in the rat race with profession and peer group. We take a lot of punishment getting there and staying there at any price. From time to time Providence permits us a glimpse of the moral and human wreckage that lies in the aftermath of the man who can claim "I am number one." Church, state, and home suffer from this despot. He is the anti-Christian.

The first reading condemns this arrogance because it persecutes the just and peaceful man whose values are its countersign. "Let us ridicule the just man because he is obnoxious to us; he sets himself against our doings." In the second reading James lashes the arrogant worldly: "What you desire you do not obtain and so you resort even to murder." He damns the "inner cravings" of those who must be lords of all. These are the cravings that push men to war, conflict, dispute, envy, desire, and consuming self-gratification. They are flames that fire men up, and eventually consume them. On the contrary, true wisdom is innocence before God and its fruits are peace, leniency, docility, compassion, kindly deeds, impartiality, and sincerity.

The Gospel presents, in the clearest manner possible, Jesus' teaching that self-glorification is the antithesis of the Kingdom. "He took a little child, stood him in their midst, and put His arms around him." There is only one Number One. His alone is all glory. He is the Father. All of us are His children. Every day that is not for us the day of the spiritual child is a day without grace. To reinforce the point He says to the Apostles: "If any one of you aspires to first place, he must remain the least of all and become the servant of all."

This most fundamental spiritual teaching in the theology of the Kingdom seems lost on many Christians. But the Church is always conscious of it. She calls her canonized saints "the servants of God." And the Holy Father's official signature is "the Servant of the Servants of God." This is what being number one in God's poll is all about.

A WORD TO THE COUNTRY CLUB

Readings: *Numbers 11:25–29; James 5:1–6;*
Mark 9:38–43, 45, 47, 48

It is interesting to listen to older priests in the arch-diocese recount the troubles they and their predecessors had establishing Catholic parishes in the Southland. Like Blacks, Jews, and all minorities, they were extremely unwelcome in several prestigious cities. It is a toil and trouble worth remembering in their favor when they are glibly dismissed as the "bricks-and-mortar" generation.

They were victims of the country club, a term whose transferred meaning has come to represent the upper echelon of prejudice—as in White Rhodesia. Its roots are deeper than the desire to live well, eat well, and play well. It grasps the substance of wealth and power which no one else may share. It lives beyond the reach and control of civil man while claiming to display the essence of civility. Every nation has this club, every society, every city. It stems from a godlikeness condemned in Genesis under the symbol of the Tower of Babel.

Even the Church is not without men and women who crave the country club, however hazy their perception of it. They want to make even the Church into Our Thing and Our Cause. She cannot be shared with others. Everyone else is minority before their exclusivism. Like racists of a decade ago, they shout "Hold the line," "Keep them out," "Stop them." In the first reading, some men not of the camp of Moses have received the spirit of prophecy. General Joshua is appalled. "Stop them, my lord Moses, from prophesying!" Why? Because they do not belong to our country club! "Would that all the people were prophets" is the reply of Moses. "Would that the Lord might bestow His spirit on all!" Would that we not set ourselves up as exclusive of others' creed, color, culture, sexual and social condition!

James, in the second reading, has severe words for the rich who exploit the poor. We can read this passage in light of our own present conditions. There are many means besides riches through which we may be accused of controlling and exploiting others—by the arrogance of our office, our intellect, our envy, our enslaving and selfish love. Bleeding the goodwill and dedication of Church volunteers and employees is especially obnoxious.

In the Gospel, Jesus is confronted with the country-club mentality in the person of John (of all people). "Teacher, we saw a man using your name to expel demons and we tried to stop him because he was not of our company." Jesus answered, "Do not try to stop him . . . anyone who is not against us is with us." Obviously, the work of God is being accomplished, and the Spirit of God is active outside the Church as well as in it, outside our apostolate as well as through it. Let us not put chains on God's liberality for the sake of promoting our little country club.

The Gospel should speak strongly to us of ecumenical dialogue and cooperation. It should speak to us also of the validity and power of the "secular" wisdom, grace, and prophecy. They, too, are the fingers of God renewing the face of the earth. It must not threaten us that others "not of our company, not of the camp" are promoting the Kingdom on earth. What should threaten us is our inactivity in that work because we are bent on limiting grace and salvation to our mentality and doing it alone. That is, whether we know it or not, an attempt to reduce the Kingdom of God to an exclusive country club—ours.

Cycle B   Twenty-seventh Sunday in Ordinary Time

IN SEARCH OF UNITY

Readings: *Genesis 2:18-24; Hebrews 2:9-11; Mark 10:2-16*

At first glance, the readings this Sunday seem unrelated. The first and third speak of marriage, while the second recalls the suffering and death of Jesus in our salvation. To compound matters, the Gospel ends with the little children whose dependence and docility are the mark of the Kingdom.

If we realize, however, that the Letter to the Hebrews (second reading) is a plea to Jewish and Gentile Christians to live together in harmony, the theme of all three readings is clear. It is a plea for union and unity.

And do we ever need the union of minds and hearts in marriage and in the Church!

Man is made in the image and likeness of God. Man is made in two complementary forms: male and female. Neither one alone reflects the inner unity of God. Together, in marriage, they do. Add a child—fruit of their love—and you have family. The family reflects in man the Trinity of God. It should not surprise us, then, that marriage and family are sacred because of their reflective theology. It should surprise us, however, that they are so casually dispensed with and so casually prepared for in our so-called spiritual culture.

Many things might be said here that are valid. We need better and more intensive marriage preparation. Young couples need assistance, especially in the early years. A sound sexology is crucial to all. Divorced Christians should be encouraged to submit their cases for review: the present legislation offers much hope for annulment of defective first marriages. Unity in marriage is served by deep communication; the Marriage Encounter apostolate facilitates this.

St. Paul, in the second reading, tells the Jewish converts that they must learn to grow in unity with the Gentile converts. Communication here is served by remembering that all became brothers of Jesus and children of His Father through His suffering. It was in the same suffering that Jesus "perfected Himself." We cannot expect union and perfection in Church or marriage without the suffering that hones the edges off our egotism, our inflated self-affirmation, and our superiority. Too many of us insist on having our own way in marriage and in the Church community. Surrender a little and suffer a little; it's good for everything, including the soul!

Like marriage, the Kingdom cannot be taken with violence. Both are graced conditions. They cannot be grasped by despots. Scheming and selfishness destroy them. We need the docility of the children whom Jesus loved so much. Approaching marriage or the Kingdom, it is necessary to put your hand in another's and enter in with faith, trust, and a lot of willingness—which is the old and the best word for love.

Cycle B   Twenty-eighth Sunday in Ordinary Time

LIFESTYLES

Readings: *Wisdom 7:7-11; Hebrews 4:12-13; Mark 10:17-30*

Doing your own thing is "in" in a big way. There is no doubt that the number and variety of lifestyles is one of the cultural explosions of our generation. You can view this as tragedy or joy depending on your perspective. It's manna from heaven for novelists and moviemakers. Variety is the spice of life; and what variety and such amounts of spice do we not have today!

Other observers see it differently. The moralist, for example, sees nothing more here than the Ten Commandments broken down into lifestyles—and validated once again. By breach rather than observance, of course.

Everyone is singing the praises of his or her lifestyle for its freedom, its grooviness, its soul, and its hitting of the mark right where I am. Well, not everyone. Critics say that Catholics, priests, and nuns are not singing at all. At any rate, the readings this Sunday present once more to our modern eyes the attraction of God's word in the matter of lifestyle.

The first reading speaks of the fundamental of any and all lifestyles. It is wisdom. It means the gift of God through which we are able to manage our lives with both insight and practical skill. Solomon is speaking with experience when he says that this gift is to be sought "before wealth or health or beauty." Without wisdom, wealth and health and beauty are no better than added weights upon our shoulders pulling us down to early disappointment.

The second reading gives us the yardstick by which we are to judge the worth and the permanent value of the lifestyle we choose. It is the revelation of God on man, life, and destiny—"the word of God living and effective . . . a two-edged sword which penetrates and divides our thoughts and our soul." We do not have to fool our life away on some kick or squander the best years on some merry-go-round. We can set our life and lifestyle by Gospel standards.

In the Kingdom as it is presently constituted, there are two basic lifestyles: Christian marriage and Christian celibacy. Through them we respond to the discipleship we engaged at our baptism in the Lord. Jesus proposes a deeper level of discipleship in the Gospel to the rich young man. It is total renunciation: "Go sell what you have, give it to the poor . . . and come and follow Me."

Nearly all the forms and expressions of Christian discipleship are under fire in the free-wheeling present age. The only real sadness here is that the fire is within the camp as well as on the outside. Christians are looking at their vows of marriage, celibacy, poverty, chastity, obedience, commitment, and dedication. They are taking a hard look at them and a hesitant look. "They were completely overwhelmed with this. . . . Jesus fixed His gaze on them and said, 'For man it is impossible but not for God. With God all things are possible.'"

Where do you stand in these matters, especially your own Christian lifestyle and your personal commitment to it? And do you still believe, with Jesus, that "in God all things are possible"?

Cycle B   Twenty-ninth Sunday in Ordinary Time

SERVICE: OUR PRODUCT

Readings: *Isaiah 53:10–11; Hebrews 4:14–16; Mark 10:35–45*

"Service is our most important product." Servant is our basic definition. This is the meaning of "ministry," and it has many forms. A Christian husband serves his wife. A Christian wife serves her husband. Parents and children serve one another. The Christian priest serves his community. The Pope is the servant of the entire Church. The particular service or ministry we perform in the Church depends on the vocation we are called to. But all are called and all are servants of the word and grace to each other.

Characteristically, the first reading is one of the Servant Songs of Isaiah. It refers to Jesus, the "suffering servant" of Yahweh. It not only projects service as the mark of the Messiah, it also projects the aspect of self-denial and suffering as an integral part of Christian ministry. "Through His suffering My Servant shall justify many." The pains and the pressures of our service are integral to its success. Let us think about that.

In the second reading, St. Paul assures us that our Christian service is not a triumphal thing. It can wear us down. It can bring the tears of disappointment and failure. We are not supermen or bionic women. It is all right to weep over Jerusalem as well as over our frailty. "For we do not have a High Priest Who is not able to sympathize with our weakness, but one Who was tempted in every way that we are. . . ." Then he adds, "Let us draw near the throne of grace with confidence to receive mercy and favor and to find help in time of need."

Who are the great ones in this life? Who are the heroes and heroines of the Book of Life? We expect children to name their favorite football player and their favorite comic strip. It is pathetic to hear adults name movie stars and corporation management. It shows where their scant culture is. Even the more intelligent among us tend to name figures from the world of politics and diplomacy, from the world of the barons and baronesses, captains and kings of money, oil, industry, and commerce.

One wonders if the common man and woman will ever learn any lesson from the lashes of history. The Apostles hadn't, so Jesus tried once again, this time with the disposition of His own Kingdom in mind. Let us pay close attention to Him: "You know how among the Gentiles those who seem to exercise authority lord it over their people. Their great ones make their importance felt. It cannot be like that with you. Anyone among you who aspires to greatness must serve the rest; whoever wants to rank first among you must serve the needs of all. The Son of Man has not come to be served but to serve—to give His life in ransom for many."

Is that my attitude and activity as a disciple of Christ? Service *is* our most important product.

THE SIGHTED BLIND

Readings: *Jeremiah 31:7-9; Hebrews 5:1-6; Mark 10:46-52*

There are constants that do not change. We forget this in an age of change. It frightens people when they hear that everything is changing; that all is in a state of flux; that to grow is to change, and to arrive at maturity is to have changed often. Spiritual qualities do not change: they simply lessen or intensify. Kindness is one of these constants of the Christian lifestyle. The people of the village where I grew up had a saying: "The true priest is the kindly priest; no other glory or failure is his monument."

I suppose this wisdom comes out of their long human experience with priests. It is rooted in the Old Testament, which affirms over and over that "our God is a gracious God, kindly and full of compassion."

The first reading is from a section of Jeremiah (chapters 31 and 32) known as the Book of Consolation. Here the God of kindness and compassion leads the remnant of Israel out of the Babylonian captivity. Note the elements that make up the remnant of Israel: "the blind, the lame, mothers and pregnant women." These are the most vulnerable people, but Yahweh is "a Father to them." Today, the deformed and the pregnant are again vulnerable, this time before the increasingly hostile laws of the lords of this earth. Our support, as Yahweh's support, must be for them.

Paul, in the second reading, speaks of the priesthood of Jesus. Here we note that the Christian priest "is able to deal patiently with sinners and the erring because he himself is beset by weakness. . . ." May we remind ourselves that priests are not gods; that they too are sinners who must "make sin-offerings for themselves as well as for the people." How genuine is our grasp of this fact? How acceptable in God's eyes are the "shock" and the "scandal" we profess at some priest's foolishness or failure? Why continue the pretense that they are angels, and worship them like graven images? Do we pray for them? Pray that they be kindly like Yahweh and compassionate like "our great High Priest, Jesus." This is the core quality on which they will be judged, and the only memorial by which they may be remembered.

In the Gospel, the cure of the blind Bartimaeus is not recorded with the usual drama, gestures, and admiration that attend Our Lord's miracles of healing. The scholars suggest a reason for this change. In this instance, the Gospel does not wish to emphasize the cure of physical blindness but rather the blinding faith of Bartimaeus. "Lord, that I may see!" Jesus answers: "Be on your way, your faith has healed you."

Let us pray: Lord, that we may see each moment, good and bad, of our lives with the eyes of faith; may we be a healing to others with the touch of our kindliness.

Cycle B   Thirty-first Sunday in Ordinary Time

A DIFFICULT BALANCE

Readings: *Deuteronomy 6:2-6; Hebrews 7:23-28; Mark 12:28-34*

"Getting it together" is a maxim of the present moment. It means different things to different people. It all depends on "where you are coming from" and "where you want to go." Love is one of the great slogans of our culture. Everyone shouts about it, sings about it, and claims to offer it. Somehow we sense that love is the healing and uniting dynamic of the human and social quest for togetherness.

Having said that, we really haven't said very much. The quest for togetherness needs more than the sense of love. It needs the definition. Christians find this definition in many passages of the Scripture. They also find its real life model in the person and activity of Jesus of Nazareth. He is not only "the Way, Truth and Life" of eternal salvation but also of love on this earth and in human interrelationships. Jesus is true love personified, and we learn the meaning and the expressions of true love from familiarity with Him—not from the Mamas and the Papas of our culture.

True love is transcendent. That means my love reaches beyond my selfishness and beyond the social sphere to the ineffable Father of all. The first reading teaches: "You shall love the Lord your God with your whole heart, and with all your strength, and with all your mind." Saints take that seriously: do we? True love is also social. In fact, we cannot bypass others and simply "go straight to God." The second reading recalls that Jesus ascended to the Father only after "passing through the veil of our flesh"; after dying from an excess of love for men and women.

The Gospel unites these vertical and horizontal dynamics of true love as a single commandment and as the essence of worship. Worship of God is empty and vain without love of Him and love of His children at our side. A balancing of these two core expressions of Christlike love is difficult. We tend to be top-heavy with the one or the other. We may spend all our time and attention, so to speak, on God while ignoring our love obligations toward His children—especially if these children are black, or brown, or yellow, or white, or poor, or drunks, or corporation captains, or doves, or hawks, or feminists, or male chauvinists!

On the other hand, we may be so "gone" on the social gospel and so "hyped" on the oppressed of the earth that we oppress God by our silence and lack of attention to Him. God does not invite us out of self-centeredness to love in order that we latch ourselves to an exclusive piety or to an exclusive "socialism."

There is no easy accommodation to loving God with all our hearts and loving our neighbor as ourselves at the same time. It is a gifted balance to be prayed for even as we try to practice it.

Cycle B   Thirty-second Sunday in Ordinary Time

WE GAVE AT THE OFFICE

Readings: *1 Kings 17:10–16; Hebrews 9:24–28; Mark 12:38–44*

Charity is problematic for most of us. Every downtown rectory has its nightly line of transients and winos. The transients are always embarking on a lengthy journey that requires a tank of gas plus. Bakersfield and San Diego are favored destinations! The winos ask only a dollar. It's for a hamburger! They haven't eaten all day and could eat a horse. Even if you respond to their requests "in charity," you still know you haven't answered their more basic needs.

In the suburbs it's a bit different. The seeker at the door is suave and polished. He's the Organization Man with the worthy cause, the big project, the shaming appeal. You watch him from the curtain and—should his cause be worthwhile—hope he sees the United Way Giver seal on the door. When you fumble and open the door at the wrong time, you try to head him off with "my husband takes care of this at the office." All in all, we want to give and we want to be generous but charity is frustrating.

The readings today take us beyond the doorbell stage and into our hearts. They offer three expressions of charity that reach way beyond the giving of alms to core Christian dispositions.

In the first reading, we have a young pagan widow with a child in the middle of a famine. Elijah makes a terrifying request of her: "Share your last morsel of food with me!" She does, believing that Elijah's God will somehow bless her and her child. She puts her life on the line in charity. She was a pagan. I am a Christian. Am I so disposed?

In the second reading, Paul tells us that Jesus gave His life for our sins. Why? Because the blood of dumb animals cannot be a sufficient substitute for our blood. Jesus, one of us, sheds His blood (i.e., offers His life) in atonement for our sins. Are we disposed, in turn, to surrender our lives for others' salvation? Too much, we say. The Christian missionary contradicts our selfishness.

In the Gospel, yet another example of charity is given us. Jesus is watching people putting alms into the collection box. He calls His disciples over to see a widow putting "two coins worth about a cent" into the box. "I want you to note that this poor widow contributed more than all the others. . . . They gave from their surplus wealth, but she gave from her want, all that she had to live on."

Let us note these three expressions of profound charity: the widow who risked her life, the Christ Who lost His life, the widow who gave her last security. Let us ask the Lord for these inner dispositions even if He never asks us for their actual expression. They will make light of the hassled feeling we have when juggling with the tank of gas, the dollar, the United Way seal, and whatever it is that's supposed to be taken care of at the office.

Cycle B   Thirty-third Sunday in Ordinary Time

PEOPLE WITH A FUTURE

Readings: *Daniel 12:1–3; Hebrews 10:11–14, 18; Mark 13:24–32*

All of us like to make estimates. So do businesses, pollsters, and analysts. We like to gauge the value of our property or the condition of our various interests. We have been looking at the Church for a long time now, estimating Her condition and making various projections on Her future and the future of Her institutions and offices.

Two years ago I stood at the entrance of my old seminary looking up at the windows as night fell. About a third of the student rooms were lighted. The priest beside me looked at the same windows and said: "It looks like we are a dying breed." In our time all those windows were alive with seminarians hard at work. In the same vein, I have heard people say "the Church is finished" and "the end is upon us."

Today's readings have to do with "the end" but not in any fearful, vindictive, or judgmental way. All refer to the eschaton—the "end of time." They are statements about our future, about our election, about our glory. They point the future with hope. Let us not sell our future short!

Before we make a mess of these readings, let us be aware that the language used is apocalyptic language. It is symbolic language, full of double and veiled meanings. It does not admit of chronological and exact descriptions such as those foisted on us in the electronic and print media by sundry "doctors" of prophecy.

In the first reading, Daniel is encouraging the Israelites not to fail Yahweh by surrendering to the pagan Syrian gods. Those who remain firm in Yahweh "shall live forever" while those who fall for the pagan values "shall be an everlasting horror and disgrace." The message for us is the everlasting life which is ours by standing fast in our Lord (Yahweh) Jesus. It is an offer of hope and future in a confused age.

In the second reading, Paul reminds us of the immovable hope that is ours in Jesus because He has already taken "His seat forever at the right hand of God in Heaven." We are "being sanctified" for this glory even now on a confused earth. In much the same way, Mark is not speaking to the persecuted early Church of doom but of hope. This is the thematic context in which he records the promise of Jesus that this present world of sin and suffering and stupidity will pass away before the saving words of Jesus and the saving Word that is Jesus.

We are a people with a future. The future is ours because the future is Christ's. We are, in fact, the only people with an assured future. Instead of estimates of gloom and doom, our estimate should be hope and future. As Paul says in another place: "Act like the Elect of God!"

Cycle B   Christ the King

JESUS IS LORD!

Readings: *Daniel 7:13-14; Revelation 1:5-8; John 18:33-37*

It is the last Sunday of the Church year. The Church, faithful one, shouts to the whole earth that Her Jesus is Lord and King. And each year She is closer to Her final union with Him. For He is coming to meet Her out of the future even as She pilgrims Her way to Him.

As last Sunday, so today: the readings look to the future, and they look to that future through the veiled language of vision and apocalypse.

Historically, Daniel (first reading) is goading the Israelites to look to the future; to hope beyond the calamity of the moment. Some day the Son of Man (Israel) will shake off the yoke of Syria and receive "power and dominion and kingship." In later interpretation, the Son of Man represents the Messiah. Later still, the first Christians interpret the Son of Man to mean the glorious Christ at the head of His people. For all the present suffering, we shall yet overcome!

The second reading proclaims the final victory of our hope in Christ. Through all the convulsions of history; despite the crimes of godless tyrants; beneath the faithlessness of institutions and the frailties of the faithful, the redemption of Jesus is moving inexorably to its appointed conclusion. He is the "alpha and omega" of all things, the Lord of time, of history, and of humanity. His Kingship simply cannot be denied.

When shall the Kingship be fully realized and manifest to all? At the end of time, says the Gospel. For it is not a Kingdom of this world. It is a Kingdom of "truth and life; of holiness and grace; of justice and love and peace."

Should we, then, wash our hands of involvement with the "social gospel," of involvement with building the better world and the new earth? By no means. There is a connection in the theology of the eschaton between the spread of the Kingdom of God on this earth and the timing of the Second Coming of the Lord Jesus. Enough to say that our wholehearted imitation of the earthly life of Jesus makes real His Kingship over our hearts here and now while also hastening its manifestation when time has run its course.

MAJOR FEASTS

Cycle B   Immaculate Conception

HUMANITY'S NEW SONG THROUGH MARY

Readings: *Genesis 3:9–15, 20; Ephesians 1:3–6, 11–12;*
Luke 1:26–38

Recently, we have been confronted again with the savagery of man toward his fellowman in the graphic productions of *Holocaust* and *Roots*. These are dramatizations of comparatively recent brutalities. We are both blessed and traumatized in our educated generation in that we are capable of a long and deep perspective on human history.

We are more aware than ever, through media, of the scope and density of "man's inhumanity to man" down through the ages. We are becoming all too familiar with individual and collective sin, with appalling crimes committed by individual persons and whole nations. The Jews were not the first people earmarked for systematic liquidation and, outside of a radically graced humanity, they shall not be the last.

The Scriptures are much more concerned with collective sin than with the singular sins of individual persons (a point poorly taken by us, perhaps, in the recent past). Today's first reading reminds us that all mankind is subject to sin since the Fall. We are permeated with it. It reaches like a cancer into the marrow of our personal and national bones. But in the offspring of one woman this permeating cancer can and will be crushed. In Mary's Son the whole wide world will "sing a new song" (responsorial) of liberation from sin.

Mary's role in our redemption is, then, far more substantial, heroic, and universal in stature than the pious theology we have encased it (and her) in. This woman is unique and pivotal to the divine plan of salvation and to our predestination in Christ (second reading). She is more than the modest maiden we bring to bear threateningly upon sexually curious teenagers and the madonna of the home we invoke to confront the wayward family man and woman.

Today's feast celebrates Mary's preparation for her august vocation as bearer of man's Liberator. She herself is conceived and born without the universal cancer of sin touching her. In this she is the first expression of the end of the cancer of sin. It is for us, reborn in the Son she bore, to expand that expression in ourselves, in individuals, and in nations until sin and sin's inhumanity are crushed.

Then, God willing, a future generation will have a long and deep perspective on a new human history that no longer shows man's inhumanity but his graced humanity toward his fellowman.

Cycle B   Presentation

PRESENT, LORD!

Readings: *Malachi 3:1-4; Hebrews 2:14-18; Luke 2:22-40*

"May I present . . ." How well we know the presentation! Less formally, TV presents us with personalities we emulate and personalities we can do without. Graduates are presented. So are debutantes. So are football players. Even Red China has been "presented" to us recently according to the godly TV estimate.

We.do a lot of presenting ourselves. "May I present my wife, my husband, my daughter, my son, my dissertation, my script, my expense account. . . ." I'm sure the presentation Our Lord really wishes to hear from me is: "May I present *myself* to You, Lord?"

Jesus was presented without reservation to the Father in the temple. Such was the Law. We, being Christ followers, must present ourselves similarly in the law of love. Presentation is consecration. "Behold, this child

. . . set for the rise and fall of many in Israel!" We present ourselves for a purpose.

Today is the day for renewing our baptismal presentation, this time with adult awareness and fervor in the decisive promise to be the servant of the Lord to His people.

Cycle B   St. Joseph

THE MAN OF MARKED FAITH

Readings: *2 Samuel 7:4–5, 12–14, 16; Romans 4:13, 16–18, 22; Matthew 1:16, 18–21, 24 (or Luke 2:41–51)*

Joseph "the Quiet Man." Joseph "the Just Man." Joseph "the Caring Man." Was he the "strong, silent type" so much admired by many women over the ages? Or was he, given the strange circumstances of his married life, a man to be scorned by other men then and now?

We know so little about him. We could attempt to flesh out the character of Joseph using the psychology and culture of his time. We could attempt to build him on the base of the few etchings the Scriptures offer of him. Either process would, necessarily, submit him to conjecture and maybe caricature. And that is the trouble with the constructed "biographies" we have of the man.

We know this much: Joseph was a man who grew up quite normally, planned to marry, selected the woman, was engaged, married, and intended a typical family life. Toward the troubled Mary he exercised concern, care, "uprightness," deference, and exceptional sensitivity (given the severity of the Law). His obedience to "the angel of God" was direct and immediate. His fidelity as a family man was heroic. But each of these characteristics is but part and reflection of his magnificent faith.

Joseph is, above all else, the exemplar of the kind of faith extolled and commended in each preceding generation from Abraham down—total faith and trust in Yahweh.

Is he a "man for our time"? Not, indeed, if a playboy philosophy is the wisdom of the age and fidelity (faith has many levels to operate on) a blight. Yes, indeed, if a playboy philosophy is human blight and a worthwhile life lies deeper than the nearest superficiality and the latest "liberation." Joseph is a great sign of contradiction to this age in its philosophy, and to each of us who plays the game of "hanging loose" with our religion or our commitments.

Joseph, the man of marked faith and simple trust, is a question placed before every Christian today, a question about the depth of our fidelities and the quality of our responses. He and his life are a challenge to our caring, our concern, our sensitivity toward others, especially those "in the household." Joseph, with his humility, sensitivity, faith, good works, and love, is a call to each of us to stir up the kindred graces in ourselves, to live quietly but daringly out of them, to accept a difficult present, and to have the hope of our future.

Joseph is a contradiction to most of the secularized culture and to much of the present Church as it enfleshes itself in its members. We are too loud, too abrasive, too critical, too insensitive, too easily self-defensive, too demanding, and too much lacking in quality faith. Joseph calls for depth in all we are and do. It is "down there" we find the liberation we seek in superficialities.

Cycle B   Annunciation

GOD CALLS

Readings: *Isaiah 7:10–14; Hebrews 10:4–10; Luke 1:26–38*

The Annunciation of the long-awaited Savior is also the invitation offered to Mary to respond to the Lord God in a unique and startling way. We know the story well, and we know her attitude and response.

We could say much about her "fiat" as the Yes that began our salvation, her response that turned the world inside out. All honor and gratitude to her!

We could say much about some forms of popular piety, which seem to lessen her stature and her true theology; and, I suppose, we could say quite a lot against those who minimize her pivotal position in presumed protection of her Son's magnificence.

All these points are worthy of treatment as full homilies.

But the point that touches me most today is the issue of invitation. God invites each of us to be Christ bearers with Mary. He invites our hearts to be the womb of His Son in our own time and place. He calls each of us to bear the Word and to offer the Word to others in special ways according to the vocations and circumstances He has given us. Let us honor Mary best by looking on our

131

vocation in life as the divine invitation to which we have given our own "fiat."

Let us stir up in our hearts the grace of our calling as Christians, as Christ bearers, as birthing places of the Word, as Christian fathers, mothers, priests, religious, workers, and whatever.

Our age grows cold from unanswered calls, broken invitations, and fading commitments. We must begin again to say Yes to God's calls and not be afraid of the response to His Annunciation: "Be it done unto me according to Your word!"

Cycle B   Ascension

THE WAY TO GO

Readings: *Acts 1:1–11; Ephesians 1:17–23; Mark 16:15–20*

I have on my desk Becker's psychology of *The Denial of Death*. Denial is one attitude to adopt in the face of our inevitable destiny. There are others, of course, some stoic and some suicidal. The latter are gaining ground among us.

Kübler-Ross offers comfort with the view of a "friendly passage." But nowhere will one find so inviting a view of death as the Christian one, which we celebrate today, our Ascension to the Father.

Jesus, model and truth, "ascends to my Father and to your Father . . ." to more than passage and peace, to glory. This is our assured and blessed future.

The Ascension represents and is the final victory over death by Christ. It can no longer terminate us and erase us. It can no longer reduce even the best of us to dusty insignificance in humankind's long and populous history.

Our Lord's Ascension is prototype and power of our own. We overemphasize the "tragedy" of those who die young and teach scant ascension theology to the old we would comfort.

Today's feast has a theology of hope for them and for us, for young and for old, for those who mourn and for those who deny. Be assured that Our Lord ascended to glory and that we, being faithful, shall do the same.

Cycle B   Corpus Christi

"TAKE AND EAT"

Readings: *Exodus 24:3-8; Hebrews 9:11-15; Mark 14:12-16, 22-26*

These Scripture readings for the feast of Corpus Christi celebrate the mystery of the Body and Blood of Christ given for the life of the world. It is easy for believers to accept the realities of the Body and Blood of Christ in the forms of bread and wine. On the other hand, such faith is not at all easy for the children of science and sophistication. We remember, too, that the Jews queried: "How can this man give us his flesh to eat?" But Jesus insisted: "Unless you eat the flesh of the Son of Man and drink his blood, you shall not have life with me."

The early Christian believers in the real presence of the Eucharistic Lord also ran into trouble with the science and sophistication of the Roman Empire. It accused them of cannibalism. Today they are accused of "ritual primitivism." But all this criticism points up a consoling fact: the unbeliever rightly grasps the fact that we really do believe "it is the Body of the Lord."

What do we mean by the "real" presence of the Lord in the Mass and in our reception of Communion? All presences of the Lord to us are real, living, vibrant. He is really present to us when we turn to Him in prayer. He is really present to us in His words speaking out of the pages of the Scriptures. He is really present in the activities of the sacraments. But in the Mass He is present with a reality that includes more than all the forms of presence just named. He is present corporeally—body, blood, soul, and divinity. It is the real and the "total" Christ, if we may put it that way.

Further, there is no other known form of Christ presence besides the Eucharist in which the believer meets the glorified Lord in such an intimacy and intensity of encounter. In fact, the only meeting with the Lord that outdoes the Eucharist is the glory of our mutual presence in the afterlife. In our present pilgrim way, the Eucharist is the summit and the depth of meeting the Risen Lord.

Through the real presence, our Lord has taken care of His side of the eucharistic encounter. But what about us? When He is offering us the most intimate and intense of His presences, are we present to respond and enjoy? When we hear that regular Mass attendance has dropped nearly 40 percent, and that youngsters don't want to go to Mass, and that adult Christianity is a matter of choosing democratically between praying at home and praying in Church, then clearly the Gospel of John and the words of Jesus have no meaning for many.

On the other hand, there is one practice that shines through all the upheaval of the present and that generates enthusiasm and unquestioned response from every priest, young and old: it is the Mass. I suspect this is the special grace God has given us in our generation and its trial. We are all grateful for it. After all, it is the Mass that matters. That's something that has not been lost on the present generation of priests, even if the polls indicate that it has been lost on many Catholics and even more of their children.

Cycle B   Birth of John the Baptist

THE HERALD

Readings: *Isaiah 49:1–6; Acts 13:22–26; Luke 1:57–66, 80*

There is a venerable monsignor in our diocese who deflates many a "modern" catechetical conversation with the insertion, "I was in on the ground floor of that!" Indeed, he was. Much of the development of religious education in this nation owes its insight and impetus to him. I hope historians will give him his rightful place, especially those located far from the West Coast.

It would be too narrow a description to say that this priest was a "CCD man." He was a trailblazer. In both catechizing and initiating catechetical ventures, he was a true herald of the Gospel. What he did made him very much a good model of John the Baptist and his work. It is accidental (or is it?) that monsignor's name is also John.

John the Baptist was the herald of the gospel of repentance and the herald of the Saving Gospel, Jesus. "John heralded the coming of Jesus by proclaiming a baptism of repentance to all the people of Israel" (second reading). We, too, are called and anointed to herald both gospels to the minds and hearts of our culture and time. And surely we are called to allow the voice of the herald to penetrate our own minds and hearts as occasion demands! In line with recent ecclesiology (capsuled, for example, in Avery Dulles's *Models of the Church*), we need to see ourselves and our Church as herald again; herald of repentance, of Good News, of joy, of peace, of love, of justice, of penance and prayer. We need to use the electronic media more and more as effective heralding to match our stature as authentic herald in an age of media. ("How shall they hear the gospel . . ."—in a TV age?)

We should be sensitive to the new annual Communications Campaign of our Church. The infirm, the aged, the shut-in, the great masses of neopagans must rely in no small way on the "electronic herald." And yet, the great personalism remains: my own stature as an authentic, committed disciple is the best herald of the Good News within arm's reach of the people about me.

When we think of the rugged personality and sparse lifestyle of John the Baptist, we ought to think prayerfully and practically of our missionaries abroad. These are they who make possible the invitation of the first reading: "Hear me, O coastlands; listen, O distant peoples!" These men and women have borne the burden and heat of the centuries. Today, they are challenged by emergent nationalism and by a questioning of their value in distant cultures.

On the home front, there is a perceived need for evangelization or reevangelization (however questionable the terminology); and there is a quandary over both the size of the number of "unchurched" Americans (eighty million) and the strategies and theologies with which to approach them.

Whatever be our dominant "model" of Church or personal preference, the need of the herald is clear and the voice of the herald must be heard again in our land. May the good Lord give each of us the gifts given John: the heart of the herald and the voice of the herald. He has certainly given us the opportunity of the herald in these "post-Christian" times.

Cycle B   SS. Peter and Paul

ALL THE WAY

Readings: *Acts 12:1–11; 2 Timothy 4:6–8, 17–18; Matthew 16:13–19*

Today's Scriptures lend themselves to a number of themes. There is "a rumor of angels" in the first reading and a snatching from "the lion's jaws" in the second. Both Peter and Paul interpret their escapades as examples of God's saving hand in order that through them "the preaching task might be completed and all the nations might hear the gospel."

In the Gospel, Peter is given "the keys of the kingdom." Jesus is acknowledged as the Messiah. Our

Lord founds the Church on the rock of Peter. Faith in Jesus is expected and rewarded.

We might look at our Church with some sense of its august beginnings today. We might accept the Scripture that it is of divine charter. We might accept the fact that it is still the cutting edge of the Kingdom of God on earth, that it is rock-fast, that the authentic believer cannot do without it. We might stir up our dormant love of the successors of the Apostles and the successor of the Rock-Apostle. And we might pray with fervor for our bishops and our Vicar of Christ.

Two items are on my own mind today. One is the conviction that Pope John Paul II is a remarkable mind and pastor. I am grateful to the Lord Jesus for his selection and encourage myself and others to pray him through the martyrdom that is the life of the bishop of bishops and the servant of servants these days.

The second item on my mind is the finality of faith that these Scriptures today suggest. There is the almost strained commitment of keeping the Faith at all costs, even a suggestion of both Peter and Paul being "used" to the last—for the sake of a "philosophy." One realizes the objections raised by humanists and psychologists to the subjugation suggested by the primary Apostles in these readings.

However, all of us who believe in the Good News and try to live it find a great example in the faith, teachings, and lives of Peter and Paul. We are encouraged to be steadfast in faith, to make the preaching of the Gospel a priority in our own generation and time, and we are invited to perceive and feel the saving "angels" of God assisting us in our mission.

We need to be evangelized ourselves from our shoes up. If the total casting of ourselves into the heart of Jesus (with *no* reservations) is not experienced by us, then I suggest we shall line up with the humanists and psychologists who do not and cannot accept the finality and subjugation of Peter and Paul. We will continue to "hang loose" in faith and dedication, and all the reforms and renewals in the world will not affect our deepest psychology.

We criticize the youth and the Hollywood set for hanging loose. If only we knew about ourselves. . . .

Cycle B   Transfiguration

DO WE REALLY SEE?

Readings: *Daniel 7:9-10, 13-14; 2 Peter 1:16-19; Mark 9:2-10*

"I've grown accustomed to her face," said self-accusing Professor Higgins of Miss Doolittle, when he really noticed her for the first time. Nothing, of course, had changed in her. He had simply stopped pontificating for a moment and perceived who and what she really was. It was quite a revelation to him.

We are all like 'Enry 'Iggins—too familiar with people and life to see their reality, their depth, their beauty, their mystery, their value, and their promise. Most of all, we're too accustomed to our spouses, our Church, our vocation, our friends, and our Lord to appreciate them and see their uniqueness.

And so it was with the Apostles. Our Lord had to take them up onto a high mountain alone so they might really *see* Him. "He was transfigured before their eyes." A touch of class? A light of glory? A ray out of the future? Does it matter? They *saw* Him as for the first time, and it was an experience they would never forget. It confirmed their faith and their love of Him.

Perhaps we, too, need to go up the mountain of prayer, silence, and reflection alone with Him. There we will certainly meet a less "accustomed to" Christ as we consider in depth that many-splendored mystery now cramped in the closed pages of our Bibles and shut doors of our hearts. An hour today alone with Him will yield a transfiguration of our too-familiar Christ—and leave us very much a transfigured self.

Cycle B   Assumption of the B.V.M.

A TRUE TRIUMPHALISM

Readings: *Revelation 11:19, 12:1-6, 10; 1 Corinthians 15:20-26; Luke 1:39-56*

Mary's feast days are days I find myself asking if the present generation knows the meaning of her titles and honors and services. We ought not assume they do. What is the "solemnity" of Mary, anyway? Or her "Immaculate Conception," or her "dormition"? And now, what is her "Assumption"?

It is something that happened to her at the end of her earthly existence. She was assumed, taken up body and soul into Heaven. In the recent past, we have been greatly concerned with stressing the integrity of her virginity, her "spotlessness," and—in the present instance—with her body not being touched by sin, or clay, or worm. And these matters are fine because they bear on important theological concerns.

However, in this age of developmental psychology, it might be good for us to stress Our Lady's Assumption into Heaven as the crowning grace of a humble life and graceful growth. Here we signal that her qualities and intense union with the Father find their completion. The Assumption of Mary also heralds forth the completion of the most truly human life our nature has generated on this planet.

At once we see pastoral implications here for ourselves. We rejoice in the achievements of this sister of ours, and we are given the pattern and the encouragement for our own lives and their projected destiny.

If, then, I am to celebrate this feast adequately, I shall have to tell myself that Mary's attitudes, qualities, values, priorities, and services are to be sought out by me from the Scriptures and commentators, and that I am to set myself the task of comprehending them and assimilating them to my own way of living—now.

I am thus "assuming" a way of life that leads infallibly to my own ultimate assumption into the presence and glory of my Father.

May she wean me and my people this way today and always.

Cycle B   Triumph of the Cross

LIFTED UP

Readings: *Numbers 21:4-9; Philippians 2:6-11; John 3:13-17*

Just as the Cross has always been "a sign of contradiction," so today I view the medical symbol in the same light. The first reading records Moses lifting up the symbol and power of life—a seraph serpent on a pole. It has become the sign of the vocation and work of the healing professions. One wonders today—when one can also read the sign as symbol of death. Today, many are vulnerable before medical personnel, and not least the infant in the womb.

To be lifted up in our salvation on His pole, Jesus "emptied himself" of the glory He enjoyed with the Father and became one like us (second reading). I suspect that many of us do not really appreciate the self-emptying of Jesus or His passion and death. Somehow, we feel, it was all part of some divine game plan in which no one really got hurt. Jesus did not "act" His way through earth and death, nor was His laying aside of His glory a process He underwent as effortlessly as a king rises from a chair and leaves a room. This second reading is suggesting a radical change in the existence of the Son of God. It is suggesting that the process by which Jesus entered our history to save us was a veritable "shaking of the foundations"—His own.

The Gospel teaches that the lifting up of Jesus is effective as to our salvation and expressive in the most dramatic human form possible of the love of God for us.

Today, let us try to appreciate the depth to which Our Lord reached into His nature and existence in order to save us. Let us appreciate the depth of the love of God for us. Let us see the Cross as central to salvation and allow it to fall against the weakest and most vulnerable part of us. Let us take up our cross, whatever it be and wherever it wounds us, with a sense of our identification with Christ and not a sense of shame. Let us be wounded by it, and let us be healers through it in our lives.

The Cross is a sign of contradiction to our age, our culture, its values. Let it contradict ourselves. And let us insist—against comfortable preachers and Christians —that there is no such thing as authentic Christian living without personal identification with the Cross in our own personal lives. If we cannot find the Cross in our lives, in our parishes, in our homes, we are in trouble.

Cycle B   All Saints

TOO HOT TO HANDLE?

Readings: *Revelation 7:2-4, 9-14; 1 John 3:1-3; Matthew 5:1-12*

About the last thing anyone wants to be known as is a saint. Our culture is death on sanctity. Even being a good family man or woman is dangerous and antediluvian. I note that Roger Staubach finds it necessary to assert that he really does like sex—but only with one woman and she his wife. This football star and exemplary Christian is placed in "a kicking situation" by the media: his very outstanding moral life doesn't fit at all with what our culture wants—a "roving" quarterback among the cowgirls in North Dallas Forty.

Hagiographers, the people who write the lives of the saints, are much to blame for the rotten image we have of our saints. They are often presented to us an antihuman ascetics and cheap miracle workers. Often they appear as antiintellectual and irrational or dripping with ersatz theology and syrup.

Popular opinion places sanctity beyond the reach of a full and integrated humanity. It's only for "unusual" types.

Saints and sanctity are in need of rehabilitation today. Perhaps the best honor we can pay them on their collective feast day is our determination to set their record straight in our own minds and hearts.

Saints are, above all else, fully human men and women following the axiom "grace builds on nature." They are the men and women, the brothers and sisters whom the Church presents to us as outstanding models of humanity, discipleship, and "living Scriptures." They are not unusual or unique or in a different class. They are and they do what we are and what we do—but in an outstanding way. The Church puts them before our faces as guideline, model, pattern, encouragement, and hope in our own struggles for personal integrity and discipleship in the Lord.

Let us pray today for a new generation of hagiographers who will present the real saints and real canons of sanctity to our time so that we may happily pattern our lives to theirs, and, in the patterning, offer them our adequate appreciation and the proper honor due their marvelous personalities.

Cycle B   All Souls

REMEMBER . . .

Readings: *varied*

The human race is given to remembering. We remember good days and bad. We remember birthdays and anniversaries. We remember milestones in our lives, individually and collectively. We remember past friends and never-to-be-forgotten pets. We remember the sublime and the ridiculous, as though nothing should be lost of the space and time that weave the cloth of our history.

There isn't even such a thing as "past remembering." All is somewhere, consciously or unconsciously.

And so, we remember our dead—and pray that others will remember us.

Christian remembrance is just as fond but also far more practical. We remember "those who have gone before us" with prayers and Masses "in the fond hope" that the Lord will take them to Himself. We remember in order to act the advocate. On this day, let us remember all who have a claim on us and, in our charity, all "whose faith is known only to God."

Let us leave the apologetics aside and take our Scriptures at their word. "It is a holy and a wholesome thought to pray for the dead, that they may be loosed from their sins." (2 Mach. 12:45)

Cycle B   Dedication of St. John Lateran

THE HOUSEHOLD OF GOD

Readings: *varied*

St. John Lateran is the church in Rome that serves as the Bishop of Rome's cathedral. In celebrating this feast of its dedication, we are mainly celebrating the universal Church, which is founded on the Rock.

All the readings assigned for today are Scriptures that anticipate, describe, flesh out, and glorify the Church as the temple of God's presence and the assembly of the household of God. The readings link together sacred shrines and temples of Israel with the early Church and the eschatological dimension of the Church. It is a panorama of all that the Church of God (as a people) is now and will be in realization.

The Church is people, a special people, who usher in the Kingdom of God on earth. The Church is the new temple of the Spirit in which and from which redeeming fires are cast upon the earth. The Church is the Bride of Christ, from whom the earth learns love and through whom the earth experiences love. The Church is the vehicle of the saving Word and the channel of God's delights to a parched and withered mankind. The Church is model of living and loving, of social harmony and the equality and protection of all men in Christ.

Truly, our task—like our definition and our future —is startling. And here we are celebrating this feast full of grace—and overflowing with challenges! Shall we invite the walls to fall in and cover us, or shall we accept the challenge to *be* church?